Casualties of War

An Infantry Lieutenant in Vietnam

1LT David Hollar

Praise for Casualties of War

"An honest and heartfelt account of a young officer's journey through war and the lasting effect it had on his life."

- General Mike Williams, A 4 Star Marine Corps General (retired) who flew helicopters in Vietnam.

"Casualties of War – An Infantry Lieutenant in Vietnam is a quiet, yet powerful telling of one man's story of his time serving in Vietnam. It is worth your while to read it -- helping those of us who did not serve, better appreciate the cost that was paid by those who did."

- Donna McKinney, M.A. (Professional writing and editing), Author of over 20 children's books. Freelance writer for Lifeway Christian Resources.

"The phrase, "WAR IS HELL!" is usually attributed to General William Tecumseh Sherman. It was true before he said it, when he said it and will be whenever war is present.

Lt. Hollar found that out for himself. His mental and physical condition, present today began in Viet Nam and followed him home to his family and friends, wracked havoc to his life as he tried to put the puzzle of what was before the war to what is now, present reality and for the past 20 years.

His journey was one which none of us would want to travel, but was traveled by many of his comrades who served in Viet Nam. An intriguing life of struggle, struggle, struggle to some semblance of peace and existent."

- Gleaton Rickenbaker, M. Div., Baptist pastor (retired)

"An extraordinary reflection on the combat tour in Vietnam by an unfortunately misplaced Army lieutenant explaining, through thoughts and feelings, the long-term effects, both physical and mental, as a casualty of war."

- Colonel Neil Johnson, U.S. Army (retired) Neil served on active duty in both the U.S. Navy and U.S. Army.

Copyright © 2023 by David E. Hollar

All rights reserved. No part of this book may be reproduced or transmitted in any form or by any means, electronic or mechanical, including photocopying, recording, or by any information storage and retrieval system, without permission in writing from the copyright owner.

ISBN 978-1-300-33245-9

Lulu Press, Inc.
Durham, North Carolina

lulu

Acknowledgements

I could not have written this book without the support of my wife, Sylvia. She was an encourager.

I am grateful to Kate Winter, my "Book Wizard" (www.manuscript2book.com) for her help. She made the publishing effort less difficult.

I am grateful to several of the men who were in my platoon who gave me significant input to the book including David Bowden, Robert Brown, John Cirjak, Gregg Drum, Paul James, Ted Pettengill and Chuck Snyder.

Dedication

Dedicated to Sylvia, my dear wife who endured so much because of my Army service in South Vietnam.

Contents

Acknowledgements v
Dedication vi

Introduction 1

1 - The Bible Says 5
2 - Officer Candidate School 10
3 - Jungle School 17
4 - Waiting for an Assignment 21
5 - Reporting for Duty 25
6 - Getting into the Swing of Things 38
7 - Brave Soldiers 48
8 - The Lieutenants Dilemma 67
9 - Time on Target 82
10 - Pine Ridge Fire Support Base 92
11 - A Day in the Jungle 99
12 - Kit Carson Scouts 104
13 - Yesterday, Today, Tomorrow 114
14 - Christmas in South Vietnam 122
15 - Hawaii Bound 128
16 - Rear Assignment 134
17 - Cease Fire 138
18 - Man on a Trail 142
19 - Relative Safety 146
20 - Welcome Home? 163
21 - Dying for Your Country 172

22 - Waging Peace 177
23 - The Night 184
24 - Out of the Night 197

About the Author 206

Introduction

"How do you ask a man to be the last man to die for a mistake?"

- John Kerry, 1971

In September 2005 I contacted David Bowden, one of the men in my platoon in Bravo Company, 1/2nd Regiment of the First Infantry Division. He asked me if I had written a book about my year in Vietnam. He said that I had told him when we were in South Vietnam that I wanted to write such a book. *Casualties of War* is the culmination of that 50-year-old desire. Thirty-five years passed before I tried to contact any of the men I served with in Vietnam. It began in March 2003 as the United States was invading Iraq. That war made me think of my days in Vietnam. I worked for the General Services Administration of the federal government in Washington, DC. My office was only a 10-minute walk from a First Infantry Division memorial on 17th Street. One day at lunch, I decided to walk over to it. The monument consists of a statue in the middle with plaques on each side where the names of those killed in WWI, WWII, Korea, and Vietnam are inscribed. I spent most of my time looking at the names on the Vietnam plaque.

First Infantry Division Memorial in Washington, D.C.
Red roses shape the "Big Red One"

On the way back to the office, I thought there might be something on the internet about the First Infantry Division in Vietnam. When I returned to my desk, I searched on "Yahoo" for the First Infantry Division. I found the division website and a message board associated with it. I explored some of the messages and found one referring to Captain Jerry Wilson. He had been my company commander for my first few weeks with Bravo Company. I emailed the author of the note, and he sent me Jerry's phone number and email address. I was delighted to obtain it.

I called Jerry's home number and left a message. A few days later, he called. He had recently organized and arranged the first reunion of Bravo Company in New Orleans.

Over the next few years, I contacted Bob Brown, Bob Gadd, Ron Farrow, Chuck Snyder, Bob Brown, Glenn Surrette, Jim Fletcher, Paul James, Marshal Copeland, Ted Pettengill, and David Bowden. They had all been in my platoon, and most of us were able to attend some of the subsequent reunions.

The photo on the cover is of the statues of Vietnam Veterans at the Vietnam Veterans Memorial in Washington, D.C. These soldiers survived the war and are looking back to the wall where the names of the 58,220 who died there are engraved.

American soldiers killed are only part of the casualties of that war. "In 1995 Vietnam released its official estimate of the number of people killed during the Vietnam War: as many as 2,000,000 civilians on both sides and some 1,100,000 North Vietnamese and Viet Cong fighters. The U.S. military has estimated that between 200,000 and 250,000 South Vietnamese soldiers died. The Vietnam Veterans Memorial in Washington, D.C., lists more than 58,300 names of members of the U.S. armed forces who were killed or went missing in action. Among other countries that fought for South Vietnam, South Korea had more than 4,000 dead, Thailand about 350, Australia more than 500, and New Zealand some three dozen."[1]

In addition, 150,000 Americans were wounded and 75,000 became severely disabled.

---

[1] https://www.britannica.com/question/How-many-people-died-in-the-Vietnam-War

First Infantry Division Area of Operations

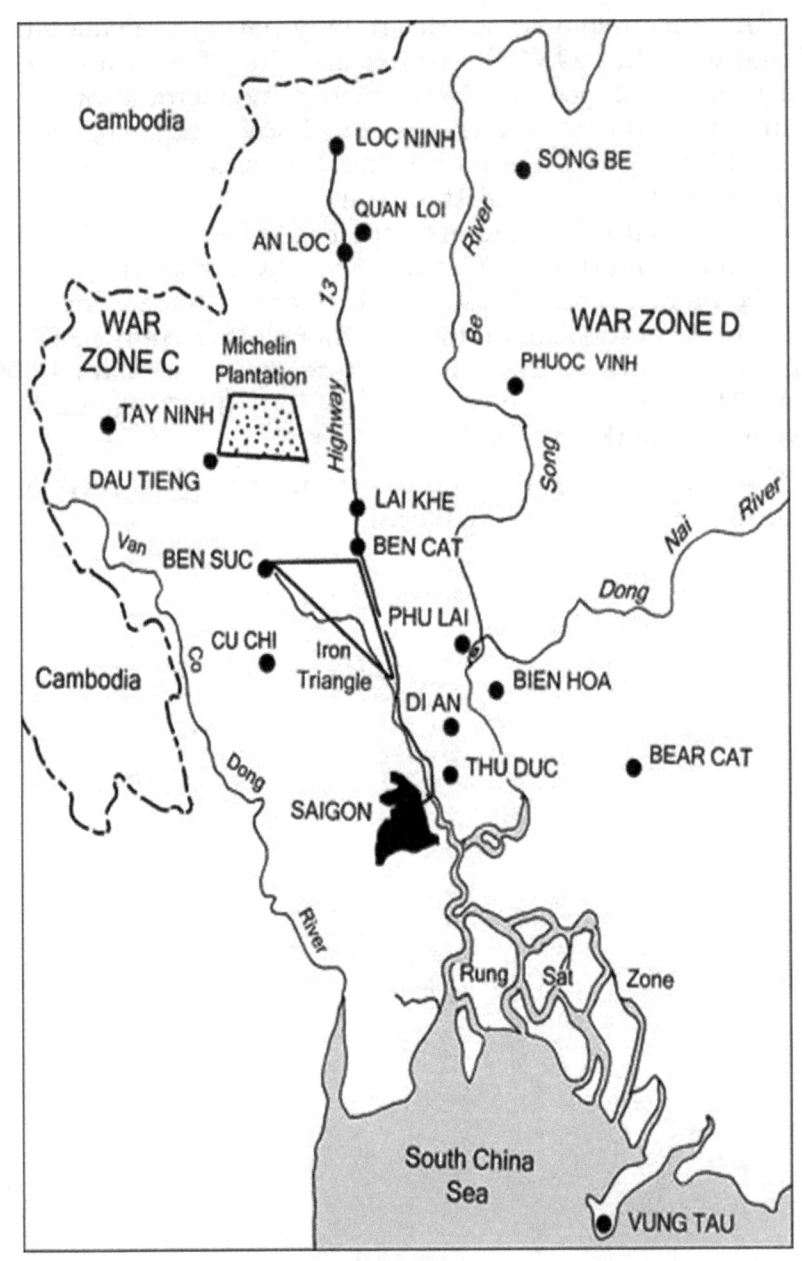

Courtesy of Joe Fair in *Call Sign Dracula*

1

The Bible Says

"War, like every other human ailment, tends to leave the body politic folded along ancient creases and festering old sores."
- WEB. Du Bois

I was born on August 26, 1944, at the Good Samaritan Hospital in Phoenix, Arizona. My parents were from Virginia, and my mother suffered from severe asthma. Her doctor suggested that she try the climate in Arizona, but it did not help. They returned to northern Virginia after a couple of years.

My childhood was typical of a middle-class household in the 1950s and '60s. My father, Charles, was a carpenter, and my mother, Grace, was a homemaker. She began working as a drug store clerk when I left for college.

I was raised in a Christian environment with my younger brothers, Paul and Steve, and we attended a Southern Baptist church each week. We were taught to be kind, honest, and loving. We were also instructed not to fight, and I do not recall ever getting into a fight with another kid. The Golden Rule was essential.

It is challenging to recover when overwhelming life events occur because one's underlying assumptions and beliefs about life are severely threatened. It requires a tremendous amount of effort on the victim's part to recover, even on a minimal level.

In my teen years, I was active in our church youth group. Most of my socializing was centered there instead of with students from my high school, which was not close to our church.

I became very politically oriented because of the threat of the spread of communism. I read everything I could find from conservative anti-communist sources, including *The Conscience of a Conservative* and *Why Not Victory* by Barry Goldwater. I attended several rallies sponsored by the Young Americans for Freedom.

I became very interested in chemistry during high school. I had a lab in our basement for doing experiments with my chemistry set. I did well in my science classes and decided to study chemistry in college. In 1962 I enrolled at Northeastern University in Boston, Massachusetts, but my grades were not good. After a year and a half, I began thinking of trying another major.

Two people from my church youth group were students at Bob Jones University (BJU) in Greenville, South Carolina. I enrolled there in January 1964 with a major in accounting. BJU was a fundamentalist Christian university with very conservative political, social, and cultural thinking. It fit me well at the time.

During high school, I began dating Sylvia Thornberry, one of our church youth group members. While I was at Northeastern, we exchanged frequent letters and dated when I was home on break and during the summer. By the summer of 1963, we were "going steady." In September, Sylvia began attending college at Blue Mountain College, a Baptist girls' school in Mississippi. She was not interested in attending BJU.

After graduation, we were married on July 15, 1967. I began working as a junior auditor at Arthur Andersen & Co., an international public accounting firm in Washington, DC. I recall my starting salary was $7,700 per year.

I remember the fall of 1966. I was a college senior majoring in accounting. Most senior guys had Vietnam on their minds, except for the young men majoring in divinity who would likely be exempt from the draft. It was a constant item of discussion, concern, and fear for the rest of us.

I took a test for a position as a cost analyst in the United States Air Force, but I did not score high enough to qualify. The competition was fierce. Since military service was a given during those years, I made the best choice available.

Service in the military did not figure well into our plans. I hoped to begin my career as a junior auditor with one of the big eight accounting firms in Washington, DC, near northern Virginia homes.

While I considered myself to be patriotic, it had its limits. The Vietnam War was not popular, and many people could not even understand why we were there in the first place. I did not want to become a Casualty of War.

Since my parents were not wealthy and did not have "connections," I had no expectation of avoiding service.

The word around campus was that a particular army recruiter in Greenville was a Christian. I went to see him try to determine what might be my best route. He told me that since I had an accounting degree and wore glasses, I would not be assigned to a combat position in the army. I was considering serving my time in the military as an officer. He told me he thought I could achieve that in the Finance Corps. However, the only way to become an officer in finance was to attend the Infantry Officer Candidate School first. That sounded encouraging, and Sylvia and I decided that I would pursue that route after graduation. I learned that wearing glasses had nothing to do with whether I would receive a combat assignment.

Sylvia and I graduated in May 1967. After graduation, I secured a position with Arthur Andersen & Co. in Washington, DC as a junior auditor.

There was much talk among the new intern auditors about military service. Some had gotten into an army or National Guard reserve unit. One of the partners was in a National Guard unit, and he put me in touch with the right people there. However, it was a Special Forces Army National Guard unit with a demanding physical exam.

I took the exam in November but did not pass. I also tried to get into several regular army guard units but could not do so. It seemed that unless you knew the right people, getting into any National Guard or reserve unit was only a dream. My choices seemed to be running out. Unlike the war we launched in Iraq in March 2003, few reserve and guard units were deployed in Vietnam. I also talked to an army recruiter near our home in Northern Virginia. He told me the same story as the recruiter in Greenville.

I received my draft notice in the fall of 1969. Sylvia and I decided that my best choice was Officer Candidate School. I relied on the recruiter's expectation to go into the Finance Corps as a second lieutenant. I felt I would have a better army experience as an officer than as an enlisted soldier.

I began Basic Training in late February 1968 at Fort Dix, New Jersey. Upon graduation, I completed Advanced Infantry Training at the same location.

Basic training at Fort Dix

Exodus 20:13 can be translated as, "Thou shall not kill." However, in the opinion of many translators, it may be more accurate to have it read, "Thou shall not murder." As soldiers, we were told that killing during war is not murder.

I was on a journey where killing would be a shared experience. The M-16 assault rifle made it easy.

I would learn that killing would not take long to become a natural reaction to perceived or actual threats. It was not difficult to decide that my life was more valuable than that of the 18-year-old Viet Cong soldier 50 feet from me.

Decades later, when I think of the killing, we did, I am haunted by the concept that killing is murder, and the Bible says, "Do not murder." At the same time, I realize that for an infantryman, killing is a necessary act to secure one's survival and accomplish the infantry's mission during the war. It is a terrible plight that is difficult to overcome. However, I found that when my life and the lives of my men were in jeopardy, the only option was to kill the enemy.

2

Officer Candidate School

"One cannot answer for his courage when he has never been in danger."

- Francois Duc de La Rochefoucauld, Maximus, 1665

I began my military service with the U.S. Army in February 1968 by completing eight weeks of basic training at Fort Dix, New Jersey. Following that, I had eight weeks of Advanced Infantry Training (AIT) at Fort Dix, graduating at the end of June. After graduation from AIT, I left for 23 weeks of Officer Candidate School (OCS) at Fort Benning, Georgia. Students were referred to as "Candidates." During the Vietnam War, the army commissioned about 50% of its junior officers through OCS. The rest were commissioned through ROTC or the Military Academy at West Point.

Over 36,000 students began OCS between 1962 and 1972. The failure/dropout rate stayed at approximately 30% during that period. Even with the increased need for infantry lieutenants, the army did not lower the standards for OCS graduation and commissioning as second lieutenants.

As reports of deaths of soldiers in Vietnam became public, the Army needed to increase its supply of infantry second lieutenants. Before the war, college ROTC was the Army's primary source for second lieutenants. That source was significantly reduced as a result of the war itself and the anti-war sentiment on many campuses. ROTC enrollment plummeted. In 1960 there were 130,000 students in ROTC, but by late 1967, it had dropped to just over 40,000. During this same period, West Point supplied only 5% of the junior officers for the Vietnam War.

I began OCS in early August 1968 and graduated on January 24, 1969, as a second lieutenant in the infantry. During OCS, we were referred to as Candidates and promoted to the rank of E-5. I was in the second platoon of the 95th Officer Candidate Company. Captain Jackson was our company commander, and Lt. Mahoney was our Tactical Officer (T.A.C. - Teach, Advise, Counsel). TAC officers were usually second lieutenants who were recent graduates of OCS.

Each training company had two chains of command. A student command duplicated the official chain. There were cadet company commanders, platoon leaders, and squad leaders. Assignments were rotated so that almost everyone served in one or more leadership positions sometime during the 23 weeks.

This late in the war, most of the men were drafted. One of the cadets who had been with the 25th Infantry Division in Vietnam wanted to become an officer and then return to Vietnam. Many thought it better to be an officer than enlisted. However, it was unusual for someone to want to become an officer and return to Vietnam. One of the cadets in my platoon was Ray Long from Alabama. Ray and I got along well, and we became good friends.

OCS was a grueling training experience. I do not have the outgoing personality that the army sought for officers. When a candidate was judged as not meeting their expectations, he would face one or more of three review panels where the brigade leadership would evaluate his work.

Two of the panels addressed leadership, and one was academics. I was required to go before one of the panels on leadership. If a candidate did not pass the panel evaluation, he could be recycled to begin the course again or dismissed from the program. I was pleased when I passed the panel and continued in the program.

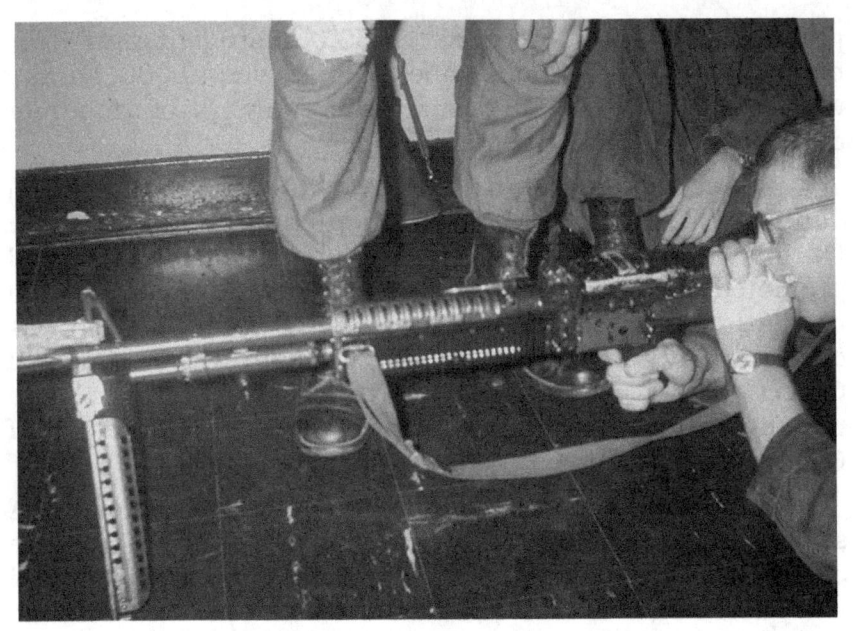

Checking out a M60 in OCS

The army determined that a good indicator of how a junior officer would perform in combat was how well he dealt with stress. It was a significant factor in the "weeding out" process. However, I agree with Ron Milam, author of *Not a Gentleman's War.*" He stated that "...combat is different from garrison, and the real test of the selection, training, and evaluation process would come in the jungle, rice paddies, and villages in Vietnam, where being an officer and a gentleman would be exceedingly tested."[2]

Lights out was at 10:30 pm, and wake up was at 5:30 am. Generally, we were not harassed during the night. I looked forward to an uninterrupted seven hours of sleep. Barracks were the same type as AIT, except two or four cadets were in a room. We had about 50 army manuals on our bookshelves above our desks.

Meals in the Mess Hall gave the Tactical Officers another opportunity to harass us. When we entered the mess hall, we were to announce our name, requesting permission

---
[2] Ron Milam, *Not a Gentleman's War*, (The University of North Carolina Press, 2009), 4.

to enter loudly. Most of the time TAC officer made us repeat it several times. He would say something like, "Cadet, I cannot hear you. Are you mute?" They often came up to us within a couple of inches of our faces and declared dissatisfaction.

After being allowed to be seated, we were required to look straight ahead, take a bite, put the fork down on the table, and repeat the sequence. There were four cadets to a table, and we were required to stand at attention until all four were present. The fourth person then called out "SEATS," at which time all of us were allowed to sit down. When a cadet finished eating, he called out "CANDIDATES, EXCUSE ME," and got up and left.

The wives of married candidates who were living in Columbus, next to Fort Benning, were expected to attend several "teas" hosted by the battalion commander's wife. Sylvia was not particularly fond of them. Formal dinners for candidates and wives were held several times during the 23 weeks.

I recall one formal dinner where Major Dempsey, the battalion executive officer, had placed name cards on the tables so husbands and wives did not sit together. The battalion commander's wife made him change them. She said: "Why are you separating husbands and wives? They hardly ever see each other." It was a welcome thoughtfulness.

OCS was continuous harassment and stress. Sylvia told me it was my choice whether I wanted to finish the course. I chose to continue.

An example of how stress was forced upon us is what I called "chaos training," when our TAC officer would announce a room change. Everyone in the platoon would receive a new room assignment. The cadet platoon leader was given only five minutes to plan the move. When the move was completed, every detail of what was on our new desk and dresser had to be the same as they were in the previous room.

My platoon decided to try not moving all the clothes from our chests but just switching the drawers into the now empty chest. It was a brilliant plan except for one thing. No one thought to look at the chests to ensure they were all the same size. They were not. The result was that when some of the candidates got to their new rooms with a drawer in hand, it did not fit into the chest. Utter chaos ensued. There was no time to go to a plan B. This taught us that we needed to plan for every possible contingency. We learned that if something can go wrong, it often will.

Harassment activities included low crawling in the grass until our arms bled up and down the barracks hallway. We also had to keep the hallway floor spit-shined. We were only allowed to walk on the center row of tiles about 10 inches wide. We were required to run until some guys threw up.

All of the harassment and pressure were to determine how well we might perform, or fail to perform, in a combat environment. The training did all it could to prepare me for firefights. However, nothing in training could genuinely prepare one for the real thing. None of our training was as horrific, disgusting, or truly emotionally taxing as was the case in a firefight. The main thing that prepared me for combat was my "baptism of fire," the first time I was in combat.

The week before Christmas, the company had what was called a ranger problem. This was a training operation in the forest designed to simulate a combat environment. We left on a Friday when the temperature was 55 degrees, but a snowstorm was predicted. Georgia was having a cold spell. One morning the temperature was only 13 degrees. One of the candidates got frostbite and had to return for medical treatment. Another candidate lost his balance and fell into a stream. Our canteens were frozen. I recall that one morning it was challenging to get my brain to determine how to move my hands because of the cold. The TAC officers were instructed that no fires would be permitted. Ours saw the folly in that and allowed a fire. He said, "You are going to Vietnam, not the Arctic Circle." We were appreciative.

At this time, Sylvia and I learned that **ONLY** the top three candidates in the class of 150 were able to choose their job classification – Military Occupation Specialty. The rest would be assigned to a military combat specialty (infantry, armor, or artillery). The majority were assigned to the infantry. Several military recruiters had convinced me that an assignment in the Finance Corps was doable, even probable. They were grossly unknowledgeable or misled me.

Had I known that obtaining a commission in the Finance Corps was nearly impossible, I likely would have chosen to enlist if I could be assured of a non-combat assignment. Options would also have included joining the Air Force or Navy since it would be highly likely that I would be in less danger than the Army infantry.

I received my gold lieutenant's bar on January 25, 1970. Sylvia, my parents, and my brothers, Paul and Steve, attended the ceremonies. My first assignment was as a training officer at Fort Benning. I would assist in training recruits who, upon graduation, would be headed for additional training and ultimately to various assignments, including in the Republic of Vietnam.

Lt. Hollar on OCS graduation day

As my class approached graduation, there was frequent talk amongst us about who would survive their year in Vietnam doing what I consider the most important and dangerous job the Army has to offer. We would talk about "so and so" and why he would not make it. Individually, we thought, "Will I make it; will I die there?"

Equally important to us was how we would respond in combat. I had what was likely the best training that could be provided for me, but the question lingered. Will I run, or will I do my job? We would not know until we experienced the first terrifying firefight. It was only then that I would know the answer.

When I was in Vietnam, Sylvia and I exchanged cassette tape recordings. On one, I spoke of whether I would reenlist in the Army. I told her I did not plan to and that the two Army recruiters' misstatements influenced my decision. I ended the tape with, "The US Army is losing a good man."

In the early summer of 1969, I received my orders for Vietnam. Sylvia and I enjoyed a 30-day leave before reporting for duty. We went to my home in Fairfax, Virginia, for that time. We took a trip to see a college friend in Akron, Ohio, and several other short trips. We were about to embark on another, longer than any other, separation because Uncle Sam said, "I Want You."

One of the exterior doors that entered my parents' home had a deadbolt lock. The top half of the door consisted of three panes of glass. One day when we were returning home, I had trouble getting the key to the deadbolt to work. My frustration overcame me, and I smashed the window with my fist. The pressure of a year in Vietnam had already begun. Before setting foot in Vietnam, I had become a Casualty of War.

3

Jungle School

"To jaw-jaw is always better than to war-war."
- Winston Churchill

As the day of departure for Vietnam approached, I became more uneasy and nervous. My Dad was about to take us to the airport. My mother was outside in the car on the morning of my plane departure. Tearfully she said something to me, which I was not able to understand. It was only later that I realized that she said, "Take care of yourself."

My first leg enroute to Vietnam was a two-week Jungle Training session at Ft. Sherman, Panama. I left for Travis Air Force Base in California from Dulles International Airport in northern Virginia.

The cafeteria at the base was open from 2 am to 4 am, so I got a late dinner. There were several second lieutenants, one of which I recognized from the 95th company.

I flew to Charleston Air Force Base and, from there, took a 4 am departure flight on an Eastern Airlines jet to Howard Air Force Base in the Canal Zone. Upon arrival at 8:15 am, about half of the 95th OCS company was waiting for our plane to take them to Oakland in route to Vietnam. Hurricane Camille was in the Gulf of Mexico at the time, and we saw the outer clouds out the windows. Cereal, scrambled eggs, sausage, juice, roll, and milk breakfast was served at 6:15 am.

From Howard AFB, it was a two-hour ride on an old school bus to Ft. Sherman. We went through the city of Balboa on the way. The humidity was terrible, and there were tropical plants everywhere. Ft. Sherman was relatively small. About a dozen buildings comprised the whole base. It was right on the northern side of the Panama Canal across from Colon, Canal Zone. I was in the Bachelor Officer Quarters (BOQ) for the first few days. There were two rollaway beds, two chairs, two lamps, shelves, and a wardrobe-type piece of furniture. There was a refrigerator in the hallway where we kept drinks.

The canal was only 15 steps from the BOQ at high tide. I could hear the small waves breaking from my room, making it sound like the ocean. Most of the buildings had no glass in their windows. They had screens with long overhanging roofs to keep out the rain. The power lines were underground since none were visible.

On Saturday afternoon, August 18, I took a nap. When I awoke, I found hundreds of black butterflies flying down the canal shoreline. You could easily catch them with your hands. They must have been flying away from rain or the wind. That evening, I saw the movie *Honey Pot* and found it quite silly.

On Sunday, we signed in, had our records processed, and were issued equipment. The equipment included a machete and an inflatable life preserver. There were 240 men in the class, with about 30% non-commissioned officers and the rest commissioned officers. Of the commissioned officers, about 15% were captains and first lieutenants. The rest were "Butter Bar" second lieutenants like myself.

On Monday, we had training classes on jungle snakes and other animals, and survival methods in the jungle. We were also taught about weapons, mines, booby traps, the Viet Cong (VC), and the North Vietnamese Army (NVA). The next day we went out into the jungle on a training operation and stayed until Saturday. The first week was "administrative," meaning we could have flashlights and fires without regard to simulated enemy conditions. The second week was tactical, and none of those pleasures would be allowed.

We went out on our training operation on Tuesday morning, beginning with jungle living and survival classes. We sampled fruits and berries that grew in the jungle and learned how to recognize the edible ones. We tasted monkey, turtle, and lizard meat. We were presented with a demonstration on how to skin a chicken. We were shown some substitutes for potatoes. We learned how to rappel down a vertical wall, which was a scary venture.

We completed a day and night navigation course on Wednesday using a compass. Thursday was a fun day. We rappelled down a 100-foot cliff, which included a small waterfall. We were divided into four or five teams, and each team made a raft out of two ponchos and grass. We crossed a 100-foot-wide river, which was 90 feet deep. Something unique about jungle rivers and streams is that they are often about as deep as they are wide, and have no banks. You step off the edge into 40 or 50 feet of water. The water has strong currents, often in different directions. We crossed one river on a rope slide and used several other rope techniques to cross the river.

It rains 160 days in the Canal Zone, and we were there during the rainy season. We set up hammocks made of a cargo net thing during the night with a mosquito net and poncho over it. It was not very comfortable, especially since we were wet all the time.

The jungle was not as hot as I expected, but the humidity was very high. I saw plenty of wildlife there. Once, an eight-foot-long snake slithered just in front of me, and there was a two-and-a-half-foot-long lizard that looked like something prehistoric.

Thursday consisted of training in ambush and patrol techniques. We came back to the barracks Friday night after a 4.5-mile hike back.

I relaxed over the weekend by hanging out at the air-conditioned Officer's Club and watching a couple of movies. I ate my meals there to stay cool.

On Monday, we began our field training exercise to simulate tactical combat conditions. We were sent out on patrols, conducted day search operations, and set up night defensive perimeters. I remembered from the first week how wet we got because of the frequent rain. This time I packed an extra pair of dry socks. I felt guilty because I changed in the evening when it was dark, and no one knew that I had on dry socks. Overall, the training I received at Fort Sherman was excellent and would prove to be very useful. Upon completion of Jungle School, I had some leave days. I came home on Saturday night, September 30. A week later, I was to report to Travis Air Force Base in California in route to Vietnam.

4

Waiting for an Assignment

"My country, right or wrong, when right keep it right, when wrong, make it right."

- Senator John Kerry

I left for Travis Air Force Base in California from Dulles International Airport in northern Virginia. The airport had vehicles that took passengers from the main terminal to the location of the planes. After I said goodbye to Sylvia, I looked out the vehicle's window and saw her. Her blue dress stood out to me. My brothers, Paul and Steve, were with her. I saw that she was looking the wrong way to be able to see me. I told the driver what I was doing and said to "not leave me." I quickly jumped off the transport and told her where I was. I wrote in a letter later, "I'm glad I came and rescued you for the single reason you were smiling when I left."

When I arrived at Travis Air Base, I had some time available before my flight left. I used it to make my last stateside call to Sylvia. I left Travis at 11:30 am. After five hours of flying with stops to refuel in Anchorage, Alaska and again at Yakota Air Force Base in Japan we landed in Vietnam. It was a 19-hour flight. I flew on an Air Lift International plane, a DC-8 commercial airline. In the 1960's airlines served authentic lunches and dinners. We had fried chicken for one meal.

We landed at Bien Hoa airbase in South Vietnam at 11:00 pm on September 4. We boarded army buses. I waited at the terminal for about an hour, consisting of a metal ceiling and open sides. The first actual indication that I was in a war zone was when a sergeant boarded our aircraft and told us that we were to take cover in the bunkers in front of the plane in case of a mortar or rocket attack. The second was seeing the chicken-wire-laced metal covering the bus's windows to keep grenades from being thrown into the bus.

The bus took us to the 90th Replacement Battalion at Long Binh base camp, where new arrivals went until they were assigned to a unit. Upon arriving, we entered a building with rows of seats with Hi-Fi playing. We were given a briefing and turned in some of our records. We converted our US money into Military Payment Certificates, which came in all denominations except pennies. They were all paper. We were assigned a bunk and issued linen. The barracks were single-floor wood construction with a concrete floor. They had showers and hot water. I got to bed the first night at 2:00 am and was back up at 6:00 am. One of my letters to Sylvia was written on September 5, where, being a plan ahead person, I wrote: "This might be a little early, but when we meet in Hawaii (for R&R[3]), remember to bring my driver's license so we can get a car."

Long Binh was a safe area, and everyone seemed to move around normally. Each barracks had sandbags around them, and bunkers were placed here and there. I heard artillery fire off in the distance during the night; I saw some flares and several helicopters. It was a quiet night, and I slept well. Usually, a new soldier arriving at the 90th battalion stays 24 to 36 hours before being assigned to a permanent unit.

We learned that brushing our teeth with concentrated stannous fluoride reduced the chance of cavities by 40%. If it was used daily, it was 70%.

---

[3] Each soldier had an opportunity to go on Rest and Recuperation (R&R) during their tour. Most married soldiers chose Hawaii so their wives could join them at the least expense.

One of the buildings had a sign reading: "If you are going on R&R, come here." I was already looking forward to the day I would be going there.

The mess hall had turkey with stuffing and all the trimmings one night. It was delicious. The drinking water tasted funny because iodine tablets were dissolved in it for purification purposes. However, I did not notice it in the iced tea. I had a lot of cokes at the Officer's Club to compensate. They also had hamburgers and fries.

Another thing of significance happened on Sunday night. I had all my money - $95 - stolen. Ninety-five dollars in 1969 had the buying power of nearly $800 in 2023. When I arrived, there was not enough room in the regular officer's barracks, so about 20 officers went to the enlisted men's barracks. Since my orders were mixed up, I was the only one in there, and I guess someone took advantage of that. A sergeant came by the following day and asked if the wallet he found in the street was mine. It was. I had the wallet in my pants pocket beside me. Nothing else was stolen. I should have locked the wallet away, but I did not. I HOPED IT WAS NOT AN OMEN FOR A COMING DISASTER IN THE JUNGLE!

On Sunday night, September 7, I asked the assignment officer why I had not gotten an assignment. After checking, they found that I had been left off the list by mistake. I should have kept quiet, and I may have spent my entire year eating cheeseburgers and drinking cokes at the replacement battalion. I learned that I would be assigned to the First Infantry Division. The division base camp was located about 30 miles north of Long Binh. According to a description of various units on the bulletin board, the First Division's mission was to defend the cities and pacify the countryside.

Officers had bunks in wooden buildings, and enlisted men had large tents with cots. Dinner in the mess hall was turkey with stuffing and all the trimmings, and was very good.

Ho Chi Minh died on September 2. I thought that would quicken an end to the war. However, in the *Stars and Stripes* newspaper, a military paper, I read that it was unlikely to affect the war. In a letter to Sylvia, I wrote: "I think it might dampen the North's enthusiasm. Anyway, I always said he wasn't needed."

Upon arrival at the 90th, I was issued a PX ration card, which limited the number of cameras, projectors, etc., that could be purchased. I received my assignment on September 10. Cassette tapes made a big difference in communication versus letters and phone calls using the Military Affiliate Radio System (MARS). I wanted to record over tapes as we made them to save money, but Sylvia thought we should keep them. That was fortunate since much of the content of this book comes from our tape letters. One armed forces station on Saigon radio played rock and roll, and I saw the news on the black and white TV in my bunk area.

5

Reporting for Duty

"...the soldier, above all other people, prays for peace, for he must suffer and bear the deepest wounds and scars of war."
- General Douglas MacArthur

I arrived at Dian, the headquarters of the First Infantry Division, on Monday, September 7. The next day my group of about 120 enlisted men and 20 officers and senior non-commissioned officers (NCOs) began a four-day orientation. We were divided into platoons with a lieutenant in charge of each. On the 10th, we went to a nearby firing range outside the base camp. We familiarized ourselves again with various weapons by test-firing each. Around noon we had a lunch break and were treated to our first encounter with C-rations while in South Vietnam. There were about 20 kids in the area. During our lunch, they went around to each GI, collecting whatever we did not want. They came up, chattered something in Vietnamese, pointed to something, and you ended up giving it to them. There was one kid, not more than six years old, just smoking away cigarettes. He knew exactly how it all was done and practiced it every day.

Our gourmet meals

The First Infantry Division had nine battalions divided into three brigades with three or four companies per battalion. Dian was about 13 miles NE of Saigon. Highway 13 was a paved road that bisected the division area. During orientation, we were told that an individual company comes into one of the in-country R&R centers, such as Dian, for three days every three months. We received additional training at Dian.

On the morning of the 12th, I completed the First Division training and soon moved to an infantry battalion assignment. After only two days out in the sun during training, my arms had acquired a dark tan.

The terrain in Vietnam varied greatly and included mountains, ravines, hills, flat land, and swampy areas. The area around Dian was very flat, and I could see a mountain in Cambodia. About a mile outside the perimeter, a refugee camp looked like a bunch of shacks.

One night the movie *The Stalking Moon* was shown. I also saw it at OCS. The PX sold issues of *Time* and *Newsweek* for four cents. They were Asian editions and were printed on fragile and flimsy paper. I also got a haircut there for 50 cents. There were girls there doing manicures while getting a haircut. Boys were also there shining shoes. I passed on both, not seeing the need for either.

My watch had a shiny metal wristband. I thought it would reflect sunlight and alert the VC to my presence, so I replaced it with a Seiko with a black leather band. I wanted to minimize the amount of shiny metal on me to reflect sunlight and attract the enemy. We had to think of everything there. On the morning of the 13th, I found myself reading James 2 in the Bible. It is about not showing favoritism and faith and good deeds. Any scripture was comforting to me.

It was discouraging writing during this period because I did not have a return address, so I would not hear from Sylvia. It was not until I was assigned to a company that I had an address.

Training included going through the gas chamber as we did in basic training. When I processed through personnel, there was a form to complete indicating whether I wanted my family to be informed of a minor injury. I wrote to Sylvia that I did, so "if I get a cut finger, you will know about it." When Sylvia and I separated in the fall to attend college, she often said, "Be good, study hard, and have fun." In some of my letters, I reminded her of those instructions. I burned all of her letters to prevent the VC from finding them and, therefore, her address. I did not want to lose any in the jungle and the enemy coming upon them and sending her harassing material.

Most of the guys left on Saturday morning, September 13, for their permanent assignments. Since S-1 (administration and personnel) had no assignment for me, I did not. It seems like I had a tough time getting positions in Vietnam.

Late in the afternoon of September 14, I was informed that my permanent unit would be to Bravo Company, 1st of the 2nd Infantry Battalion, First Infantry Division. The battalion's headquarters was at the small town of Dau Tieng, 45 miles northwest of Saigon. Next to the town is the Michelin Rubber Plantation, developed by the French. The buildings at the camp were of French design, and several were used as headquarters for the three battalions located at Dau Tieng. The Battalion Headquarters was housed in one of them. I flew to Lai Khe on the 15th on a Caribou aircraft. On the morning of the 15th, I caught a Caribou flight to Dau Tieng.

Base camp in the Michelin Rubber Plantation

On an operation in the plantation

Rubber plantation

John Cirjak at battalion headquarters

I met with the Battalion Commander, Colonel Holt. He gave me the "welcome to the unit" talk and said that no one in Bravo Company had any soldiers killed since December 1968 and that the area had been relatively calm recently. That, of course, was welcome news to me. It was significant that he thought it relevant to tell me that information. It raises an interesting question about how many Americans are told that by their new boss's boss on a new job.

Colonel Holt's wife lived in Vienna, Virginia, and he said she would contact Sylvia, who was staying with her parents in Vienna. Neither Sylvia nor I recall that ever happening.

He said it is normal for a lieutenant to be assigned to a staff job after about six months in the field. The assignments could be at the Company, Battalion, or Brigade level. Sometimes the assignment came even sooner. He invited me to attend his staff meeting the following morning at 7:00 am.

When I arrived at Bravo Company, I was issued a rifle, a map of our area of operations, and a compass. I would learn how important all were in the coming days. As platoon leader, I needed to know where we were located in regard to the map. It did not take long to realize that I was pretty good at map reading and using my compass. I had the same experience when I took map reading in OCS.

Jungle fatigues were made of a porous material so they would dry out faster. With all the rain, that was an important feature. They also had six pockets, four in the shirt and two large ones in the trousers. There was plenty of room for my map, compass, notebook, and other personal items.

I was scheduled to fly out by helicopter to the unit in the field on the morning of September 16. During the night of September 15, I got very little sleep. I would wake up every 45 minutes to an hour and be glad it was not time to go. I had many reservations, fears, and uncertainties about my future. I feared becoming a Casualty of War.

Finally, morning came, and I went to the helicopter pad. We took off and flew low over the Vietnam landscape. I was surprised that the chopper had no doors, so the passengers were in an open-air aircraft.

As a rifle platoon leader, the combat environment was a constant source of stress. I was responsible for the lives and welfare of 30 young men. What I did and how well I performed would play a large part in my men's safety. In Vietnam, there was no front lines. A guerrilla war means that the enemy can be anywhere at any time. Our front line was behind us, to our left and right, above us (snipers in trees), and below us in tunnels. The enemy was everywhere and nowhere since they were so elusive.

As an officer, I was at greater risk of injury or death since the enemy would seek out the leaders in a firefight. This fact was highlighted by Colonel Hal Moore in his after-action report in November 1965 from the Battle of Ia Drang Valley. He wrote:

> "He [the enemy] definitely aimed for the leaders -- the men who were shouting, pointing, talking on radios. He also aimed for the men carrying radios. He also appeared to concentrate on men wearing insignia of rank – particularly non-commissioned officer with stripes on his arms."[4]

As platoon leader, I would shout, point, and talk on the radio. I was a prime target for the enemy.

I was aware that I needed to be correct all the time in the decisions I made. Any failure could result in someone being injured or killed. That was an immense level of pressure being placed on a young lieutenant. Being correct just most of the time was not enough.

We landed in an open area within the Michelin Rubber Plantation, one of the areas where the battalion operated, at about 10:00 am. I asked a soldier where I could find the CO (Commanding Officer). He pointed to where he was standing.

In training, we were taught how to salute a superior officer when we had a rifle. It was performed differently than when you did not. I was to hold the rifle on the ground upright on my left side and bring my right hand in a salute fashion over to the rifle at my side. I wondered if that rule applied when in a combat situation. It seems funny now, but

---

[4] https://lzxray.com/wp-content/uploads/2015/03/AfterActionReport.pdf

that was my first concern at that moment. I decided to use the proper salute when I reported to the CO. I did, and he returned the salute but seemed a little surprised at my method. Later I was informed that any form of saluting in the field was not done.

The CO was Captain Jerry Wilson. I described him in a letter home as a real "old-timer." He was in the Marines before the Army and later became a non-commissioned officer before receiving his commission. His present tour in Vietnam was his second. He was a rough-talking man with colorful language who knew his "stuff" about surviving combat in the jungle of Vietnam. In 2007, I attended a reunion of Bravo Company in Nashville, TN. At that time, Jerry told me that before he became the CO of Bravo Company in December 1968, the company had been out in the jungle and was flown by helicopter back into the base camp only to realize that they had left a man out in the jungle. The battalion commander told Jerry to take the company back out and find the man. All they found was his boots. The NVA had captured him and taken him away. I am thankful I did not know that story when I was there in 1969.

Upon arriving in Vietnam, I knew very little about the history of the country. This was an error in Army training since it would enlighten the soldiers to a long history of oppression and invasions. Of course, such knowledge may have led to more people opposing the war. Vietnam's history is highlighted by nationalism, resistance, patriotism, and pride. Their citizens had a sense of their history and heritage: In 208 BC China invaded Vietnam and ruled until 939 A.D., when it regained its independence. It was invaded by Japan, the Mongols, France, and finally, America in the centuries following. The French came to Vietnam in 1858 with 3,000 troops as they exercised their colonial rule.

I had been sent to a country that knew about foreign invasions and dominations. No wonder former President Gerald Ford said:

> "We made the same mistake that the French did, except we got deeper and deeper in the war. We could have avoided the whole darn Vietnam War if somebody

in the Department of Defense or State had said, 'Look here. Do we want to inherit the French mess?'"[5]

After a while, the company moved out on its mission for the afternoon. We proceeded to a specified location, searching for any enemy activity. Captain Wilson rotated which of the three platoons went first each day. The two other platoons followed behind the lead platoon. My platoon was the "Mike" platoon. The others were "Lima" and "November." It was Mike platoon's turn to take the lead. We moved out, and after about 20 minutes, the CO radioed for me to return to his location. Captain Wilson said, "What the hell are you doing up there"? It turned out that I was not keeping him informed of our progress and what was going on at my location. As we continued our pursuit, I returned to the platoon and kept him informed of what we were doing, seeing, and other important information.

Men of Mike Platoon

---

[5] Gerald Ford, interview by Bob Woodward and Christine Parthemore, *The Washington Post,* December 31 2006, sec 1B, 1.

When we encountered the enemy, they were usually in groups of three to 10. Thus, we usually vastly outnumbered them. A gunship or artillery was called in to destroy the enemy. Even if it was just one VC armed with an AK-47, massive firepower was placed upon him and the route he was likely to use to escape. Usually, their minutes were numbered when we clashed with them unless they could escape. Prisoners were not typically taken because the GI would fire everything he had. This usually eliminated the possibility of any enemy coming out alive. Increasing the body count was a constant goal.

During the Vietnam War, the body count was an indicator of how well a unit was performing. Capturing real estate meant little, as was the case with the Hamburger Hill battle: The Battle of Hamburger Hill was fought from May 10 to 20, 1969. The heavily fortified hill was of little helpful value to the US. Seventy-two GIs were killed, and 309 were wounded, taking the mountain. Several days after the mountain was captured, it was abandoned. That battle became a symbol of the uselessness of the war. My company would go through the same jungle areas many times in search of the enemy. After we left, they would always come back.

Keeping track of Body Count

When we set up for the night, a forward observer would plot artillery rounds at specific points. He would identify the plots to the gunners at the base camp. If we had enemy activity, he could call for artillery to come in at those points and adjust it to where he needed it. He might radio the artillery battery and instruct them to drop 50 meters and right 25 meters. That meant that their guns would be adjusted, so that artillery rounds came in 50 meters closer from the predetermined mark and to the right by 25 meters. When he was satisfied that the rounds were hitting the enemy, he ordered "FIRE FOR EFFECT." In this case, multiple rounds of artillery would bombard the enemy. We could bring artillery rounds to within 300 meters of our location without fear of killing ourselves. I have heard of occasions where the platoon leader brought in the rounds very close to his position because the enemy was overrunning it. Fortunately, I never had to deal with such a horrible thing. If I did not have a forward observer assigned to the platoon, I would often direct the artillery fire myself.

Sometimes white phosphorus (Willie Peter) artillery or mortar rounds were used. Generally, they were used to mark locations to adjust from, but sometimes they landed among enemy soldiers. When they exploded, the burning white phosphorus would be blown out in all directions. A Willie Peter round burns at a temperature of 5,000 degrees Fahrenheit. If it attaches to the skin, it will burn right down to the bone. When referring to victims of a Willie Peter round (or napalm), the despicable term "Crispy Critters" was used. Soldiers in war quickly become calloused to death – especially of their enemies – and use such terms as "crispy critters" as a psychological defensive.

One evening soon after I joined the company, we were setting up for the night. I got a whiff of a strange odor. I found that one of the men had brought a can of bug spray and sprayed it around the perimeter of his sleeping position. Of course, such behavior could not be tolerated. The VC could smell the stuff a mile away. I reprimanded the soldier, and we spread the spray around as best we could.

A Red Cross emergency evacuation helicopter (Dust-off) was called when a soldier was wounded and was often overhead within 10 minutes. When an American soldier was wounded, every effort possible was made to get him to a medical facility. The enemy had no such care.

Anyone who persevered through basic training in the military forces is aware that the trainees' language was anything but appealing to many ears. That was my experience in basic army training and advanced infantry training. I thought I was prepared for anything that might be thrown at my God-given hearing devices. I was wrong. On my arrival in 'Nam, I quickly became aware of the unique use of the English language. I came to believe that it was a way for the soldiers "stuck" in Vietnam to release the fear, unhappiness, loneliness, and melancholy feelings of their dreaded existence for that year. The GI's vocabulary was a plethora of foul, profane, and vulgar repetitions of the "F" word, "GD," "SOB," and "MF." Often several would be used in the same sentence and were in constant use. A GI was subjected to this during his entire year in Vietnam.

As a platoon leader, I faced military matters, psychology, race relations, and counseling of men in my platoon. Race relations involved dealing with my African American soldiers' unique requirements needs. After all, back in the states, they faced significant racism. Now, they were expected to fight for their country.

When we were in the field, I did not see any animosity between them and the rest of the platoon. Our lives were on the line, and that was the preeminent concern. We worked together. When we were at the base camp, the African American troops hung out together. They were usually in groups of five or more. They had a racial bond in addition to men's friendship in combat. Both were strong ties.

African American troops hung together

Toothpick on left with his buddies

6

Getting into the Swing of Things

"Truth is incontrovertible. Panic may resent it. Ignorance may deride it. Malice may distort it. But there it is."

- Winston Churchill

On November 18, my platoon was in a night Ambush Point (AP). We would stay in that position for the night. The other two platoons were nearby in their APs. The next day we were to be resupplied by choppers and were scheduled to blow up some VC bunkers in the area. I received my Combat Infantryman Badge (CIB) on November 5. It was awarded because I had served over 30 days in combat.

A US army infantry company typically consisted of three platoons of about 30 men. Each platoon had a platoon leader, usually a 1st or 2nd lieutenant, and he had a platoon sergeant who would generally be an E-6. A platoon was divided into three squads of 10 to 12 men, each having a squad leader. When I arrived at Bravo Company, there were 32 men in my platoon, including myself. By November 22, I was down to 25 because of men wounded and rotating home after their year tour. My three squad leaders were experienced and very good. There were two E-5's and one E-4. The two E-5's graduated from Non-Commissioned Officer School. It was several weeks in length, and graduates were referred to as "Shake 'n Bakes" due to the shortness of the training. My Platoon Sergeant was Sgt. Knowles. He had 18 years of service and had been with the First Calvary Division on his first tour. The CO had Sgt. Knowles stay with me on the first day while I became oriented to things. Ted Pettengill (Doc) was our medic. He is a good man. He is from Maine and said he had a high school principal who graduated from Bob Jones University, my alma mater.

We found dozens of bunkers during my first two days in the field but only a few VC. On the 18th, Lima Platoon encountered about four VC and killed two, with the others escaping. Two days later, all three platoons met in the vicinity of a burned-out village. Lima platoon searched it for any VC activity. My platoon and November platoon remained in position nearby to see if any VC approached the village and if the Lima platoon needed assistance.

Firefights with the enemy were not our only worry. There were concerns about malaria, insects, snakes, and other threatening critters. Each day we took an orange pill to protect ourselves from malaria. In addition, we had to lug around a 60-pound backpack. The VC were experts at placing booby traps in the jungle whose goal was to maim GIs, such as Bouncing Bettys, toe poppers, punji sticks, and Chinese grenades

A helicopter resupplied the company every two days during the rainy season. It was a great morale booster for all of us. We received ammunition, clean clothes, a hot meal, and sometimes almost cool sodas. An assortment of goodies was included in the C-Rations: razors, razor blades, shaving cream, shoestring, soap, candy, gum, cigarettes, cigars, and toilet paper. C-Rations were not too bad, especially if some Heinze 57 sauce was added. It could be purchased at the base PX. A favorite was pound cake and peaches, which were worth their weight in gold. Other combinations included ham and lima beans, canned fruit, beef and potatoes, crackers, pork slices, spaghetti and meatballs in tomato sauce, and cheese spread.

When I was a platoon leader, I thought that most of the over 500,000 troops in Vietnam were doing what we were doing. I was wrong. Years later, I realized that there is something in the army referred to as the "Tooth to Tail" ratio.

The teeth are the infantry, and the tail consists of the troops supporting the teeth. No more than 10% are the teeth in a large-scale military operation. We were a minority.

The rainy season lasted about six months. It began in the north and gradually moved south. We were located in III Corps, where the season started around April and ended in late October. It ended about a month or so after I joined the company. There was rain every afternoon and most nights. The sky was usually cloudy, and the temperature was in the 90s during the day. Our jungle fatigues and boots did dry out quickly. In contrast, it could get down to 60 or 65 degrees at night. During the dry season, there would be rain every two to three weeks.

We needed to stay hydrated. I found that I needed about five quarts of water each day. However, one of the most uncomfortable and irritating parts of being in South Vietnam was the continuous rain, particularly when trying to sleep. It was terrible. I recall nights when I was trying to sleep with an inch of water all around me. It seems that everything was designed to make us miserable: rain, heat, mosquitoes, leeches, other insects, snakes, and more. One day when we were moving through the jungle, we saw a dead dragon-like creature. It was ten feet long, and its head had been crushed. There was no room for any type of vehicle to have run over it, so we expected another US unit or the VC had crushed its head with a large rock. There were a variety of life forms in the jungle. I had been thrust into a strange and new world.

Lt. Hollar in several feet of water

We could also be cold in the tropical weather when we were drenched at night. It could take all night for our fatigues to dry out, while socks would take longer. I would try to keep warm at night by covering myself with the poncho liner. There was another element designed to make us miserable. People were trying to kill us.

Bob Brown was one of the men in my platoon. His nickname was "Rebel." This is his recollection:

"I have little chronological recollection of my year in Vietnam. Therefore, I cannot tell when this event occurred, but I remember that Lt. Hollar was our platoon leader. I am not sure who our platoon sergeant was then, but I think this incident happened after SFC. "Pappy" Knowles had left the company.

"My squad was moving through the jungle just outside the Michelin Rubber Plantation when we came upon a creek we had to cross. Three of the squad (I think they were Sgt Fletcher, Sgt Snyder, and Glen "Slim" Surrette) forged across and set up an LP on the bank while another squad member and I stayed in the creek filling canteens. The remainder of the squad (three, I think), along with the M-60 gunner (David "Tex" Bowman), his assisted gunner, and our platoon sergeant, remained behind on the bank.

"Suddenly, someone from the LP called back, "Gooks." I tossed the canteen I was filling to its owner, retrieved my M-16 from whoever was holding it for me, and joined the rest of the squad as we rushed to the LP. Just as I arrived, I saw several NVA walking down a trail that ran alongside the creek. Someone opened fire, and I joined in. One Gook went down, and the rest scattered.

"After about a minute or so, a cease-fire was called. I went with Sgt. Fletcher, Sgt. Snyder and "Slim" to check the Gook that was shot. He was wounded in the leg. We called back to the rest of the squad to join us and told them we had a wounded POW. Someone came up and started to shoot the POW, but Sgt. Fletcher stopped him. We soon found a blood trail but never found the wounded Gook.

Bottom left, Beavers; to the right – Jim Fletcher, Ted Pettengill (Doc), Marshall Copeland, Paul James

"Several minutes later, Lt. Hollar and the rest of the platoon joined us. Lt. Hollar radioed the CO (I don't remember who he was, but not C.P.T. Jerry Wilson) and told him about the wounded POW. We were ordered to take the POW to an LZ to be dusted off. I remember waiting a long time for the chopper as GIs and ARVNs were given a higher priority over NVA and VC."[6]

The company returned to the base camp at Dau Tieng on Sunday, September 21. The real highlight of life in Vietnam was getting cold sodas, a shower, hot meals, and a roof over our heads. The very things that are so common and standard at home were a luxury. A cold soda could become the most fantastic thing in the world after being in the jungle for 10 days.

The base camp at Dau Tieng was some 10 miles in circumference, with defensive bunkers every 150 feet on the

---

[6] Email from Bob Brown, January 9, 2009.

perimeter. Also, the entire rim was encircled with barbed wire. At the base camp, officers and senior NCOs had beds in a wood-constructed building. The enlisted men slept on cots in large tents.

We came back into base camp on September 26 and went out again the next day. We took choppers to Fire Base Pine Ridge to secure it for a few days. Then we returned to the base to be a ready reaction force if some other unit got into trouble. Our work hours at the fire base were 7:30 to 11:30 and 1:30 to 5. We received two hot meals a day, with lunch being C-Rations. We were in a bunker, so we had a roof over our daily mail calls.

Infantry battalions used Fire Support Bases to locate an artillery battery, providing ground troops support. They would be scattered around the area of operations for the battalion. Pine Ridge was on the northern end of the Razorback Mountains, north of Dau Tieng at 900 feet elevation. The view from the base was breathtaking. Occasionally, I would see Air Force jet fighters swoop down and drop bombs. We could also watch Huey choppers insert one of the battalion's companies into the jungle. Watching from such a viewpoint gave me a unique perspective of the operation. In a tape to Sylvia, I told her that their firepower made us feel good and "a little safer."

In the jungle, we stop searching for the enemy around 5:00 pm to set up for the night. It was dark by 7:30 pm, and we usually started guard duty at 8:00 pm. Each man would pull guard duty twice each night for one hour each. There were six men in each position, so we got seven or eight hours of sleep each night. We got up at 6:00 or 6:30 am and began the day's activities at about 8:00 am. I fixed coffee most mornings. We heated our water and food by burning C-4, which came in bars. It was an explosive used to blow up bunkers. However, when burned, it made a controlled hot flame. A special breakfast for me would be coffee, canned peaches, and pound cake. When we were resupplied, the men would bargain for a can of peaches or pound cake. It was not until the 20th that I had worked up to two meals a day. I was too scared and nervous to be hungry. I was becoming a Casualty of War.

When I first arrived in South Vietnam, I would snore. Since this would alert any enemy nearby, my men would awake me and say: "Sir, you are snoring." I imagine some were hesitant to wake me, and others did not care. Anyway, within a couple of weeks, I STOPPED snoring! When I came home, the snoring returned.

On one occasion, we called for a gunship to attack some VC for us. He fired his rockets at them. The exploding warheads started a fire in the area. We had to scramble to avoid the flames. The fire only added to the heat of the 90-degree day.

We used a standard formation when we moved through the jungle on operations. The lead platoon had three elements: the scout column and two parallel columns fifty feet behind the last scout. The two other platoons would follow behind the lead in two columns. Each element had from eight to a dozen men, depending on the platoon's size.

I was the second man on the right who had a column behind the scout line. Behind me was my radiotelegraph operator (RTO), and behind him was an M-60 machine gunner. The Platoon Sergeant, his RTO, and another machine gunner were at the rear of the line to the left and parallel to mine. If the jungle was too dense, we would use one line because the thickness of the growth made it too likely that the two parallel lines would become separated. The front line of scouts would also have an RTO as the third man in the queue.

                    O Point man

                    O RTO

                    O

                    O

                    O

O.   O

O.   O Platoon leader

O.   O RTO

O.   O Machine gun

O.   O

O.   O

O Medic   O

O RTO   O

O Platoon Sgt.   O

O Machine
   Gun   O

Formation the author's platoon took when moving through the jungle. If the vegetation was too dense just one file would be used. About 50 feet would separate the lead element from the rest of the platoon. The two columns would be separate by 30 – 50 feet depending on the thickness of the jungle.

The M-60 machine gun was a critical weapon. It could lay out a band of firepower at the rate of 500 to 650 bullets per minute. It was a lethal weapon. The gun's recommended use was to shoot short bursts so the barrel did not get too hot and burn out. The gunner might not hit any enemies, but it would keep their heads down and frighten them. The enemy's equivalent was the Chicom 56 light machine gun.

Cleaning a M60 machine gun

In a September letter to Sylvia, I wrote, "I have thought I may want to take my R&R earlier while still in the field. I'd rather have the time out of the field than when I get a staff job." The total time out of the field when going on R&R would be close to 10 days. I had only been with the company for 11 days when I realized that any time, I could get out of the field was a good idea. Comfort and safety were the primary benefits.

7

Brave Soldiers

"We didn't know we were till we got here. We thought we were something else"

- Robert Stone; *Dog Soldiers,* (1974)

On the 24th of September, we were resupplied by a chopper. A Protestant and Catholic chaplain came out and conducted services. It started raining when they arrived and kept it up through the services. We choppered back to the base camp on the afternoon of the 26th. We went back out on the morning of the 27th.

On September 30, the company flew by helicopter to Fire Base Tennessee near the Saigon River, which was about 50 miles northwest of Saigon. It consists of a heavily armed perimeter with artillery set up inside the perimeter. They also had a radar tower that tracked personnel movement. On the night of the 30th, Mike and November platoons went on an ambush assignment outside the perimeter, and Lima platoon manned the bunker line. Fortunately, it was a quiet night for all of us.

Radar was on the perimeter of the battalion base camp and fire bases. They could, for example, pinpoint four persons moving north by northwest on a 320 azimuth. However, we found that there were false readings all too often.

It was getting dark when we moved out to our ambush sites. We got to where we were supposed to be. I stepped off the road to set up the first position. As I stepped off, I went up to my knees in marsh water. We set up elsewhere, and I slept wet another night. The mosquitoes were terrible. We slept with our poncho liners over our heads to keep them at bay.

On September 30, I received a much-awaited letter from Sylvia. Since talking to her from Travis Airbase in early September, I had not heard from her. I wrote to her: "I believe everyone in the platoon was happy. Sgt. Knowles said he hoped I would get one so I'd be better to live with."

On October 1, I wrote a letter to Sylvia saying, "I have decided that I never want to go camping again. I may feel different in a year from now, but now I'd be willing to have every tent, trailer, and camper burned." The following day, we went back into the firebase expecting a hot breakfast, but we were greeted with only warm sodas with a bit of ice.

I saw my first USO. Show at Fire Base Tennessee. It was a group of two girls and four men from Australia. They were pretty good and gave us a needed respite from the daily grind of war.

During the day, Chinook choppers were busy bringing supplies, ammunition, and water to the base. The Chinook had two rotor blades and was the workhorse chopper in Vietnam. It would carry supplies, ammunition, and weapons to units in the field. They brought empty water trailers back to the base camp, filled them up, and flew them back.

During dull times, I had time to read books. However, there were periods when life was everything except boring. Thursday, October 2, 1969, was one of those days.

Fire Base Tennessee was not our usual area of operation; typically, we were in areas further south and east. The order came that we were going to move out the next day. I had only been with Bravo Company for 16 days, so I was still very "green."

Captain Wilson mentioned that we might be going into a "hot" area. A hot area was where the enemy was either known to be located or thought to be. Regularly the CO rotated the platoon that would take point. That day was my turn, but he said the 1st platoon was going first. The platoon leader of the 1st platoon, Lt. Dennis King, was more experienced than me. None of the guys in the 1st platoon were happy about taking point out of turn. I thought at the time that was a little strange. The platoon leader, Lt. Bill Guide, of the 3rd platoon, had been in the field for six months or more, so he was the senior platoon leader. He was close to getting out of the field and placed in a staff job. Platoon leaders usually stayed in the field for about six months, after which we would be assigned to a staff position in battalion, brigade, or division. The staff assignment was greatly anticipated for several reasons. First, it likely meant we would be in a much safer environment. Second, we would sleep under a roof and have three hot meals daily. A third potential benefit was that I would not be directly responsible for a platoon's men's safety. That would depend on the assignment. For instance, an appointment to S-3 operations could place us in the Tactical Operations Center (TOC), which coordinates the battalion's activities in the field. Decisions there would have a direct impact on the troops.

We began our mission in the early morning of the second. Everyone was nervous and on edge. The company was air assaulted to the LZ, with Lima platoon going first. Greg Drum was with Lima and was on the first lift out. The insertion was treated as if they were dropping into a hot LZ with the chopper door gunners firing into the wood line right up to when the men jumped off the whirlybird. Upon hitting the ground, each man dashed into the wooded area, firing their M-16s as they advanced. So far, so good! To the relief of everyone, the LZ was cold; there were no enemy soldiers, so there was no return fire.

As soon as the entire company had landed, Lima took off into the jungle growth on a predetermined azimuth. A GI named Langley was on point, and Greg was his cover (keeping an eye out for the enemy). The point man was the first man in a column as it moved through the jungle, elephant grass area, or wherever the assignment took us. His job was a risky one; however, some of the men would request the position. It may have been for the thrill of being up front or, more likely, as Jim Fletcher told me at a 2014 reunion, this way, he knew what was happening since they were in the lead. It took some of the strain off because they were not somewhere back in the column, wondering where they were going. The point man was usually the first to know what was happening, good or bad.

The soldier on point was responsible for keeping the column moving in the direction the platoon leader or company commander assigned. He was focused on that task as he fought the jungle growth in front of him. That was often very difficult since the jungle was a thick tangle of vines, and it would use all of its resources to slow down or stop the column.

Langley was exposed to the enemy as he proceeded through the jungle. Greg, as his "cover," was to provide protection. He offered an extra set of eyes, searching the area to and fro, looking for anything that screamed out "enemy." If he saw something he thought was a threat, he was to alert the point man, and they would both drop to the ground. Depending on the circumstance, they may begin firing their rifles at that moment. The decision had to be made quickly as there may not be a second chance.

Shortly after noon, they spotted a latrine constructed by the NVA. It was merely a hole in the ground covered by bamboo. That discovery was relayed via radio to Lt. King and Captain Wilson. Soon after that discovery, they came upon an enemy bunker. Langley went into the bunker while Greg stood guard next to the entrance. They found ammunition, grenades, and other war-making paraphernalia. Langley handed all of it out to Greg.

Greg proceeded further into the jungle area with Lt. King close behind. They continued about 15 yards when they came upon a well-used trail split into two trails, one to the left and the other to the right. Greg took one step to the right when he heard Lt. King say, "What's that?" At that moment, a barrage of bullets streaked out of a nearby bunker that had not previously been spotted. Greg and Dennis immediately dropped to the ground. Both had been standing when a full clip of bullets (20 or more) was likely discharged in a few seconds. All had missed them.

Left to right – Lt. King, John Cirjak, Lt. Shaunassey

Greg fell backward in front of Dennis, so he was lying on his back. King began firing his M-16 on automatic with his rifle being steadied by resting it on Greg's chest. At this time, Greg was wounded in the arm. A bullet hit his "good luck bracelet," plunging pieces of it into his arm. At the same time, some of the debris from his bracelet hit him in the chest.

The firing continued for 15 or 20 minutes between the enemy and the Lima platoon. Greg had managed to position himself back on his stomach. Jenkins, another Lima GI, was to the left of Greg, firing his rifle. He was positioned such that the shells fell on LT. King.

The extended firing of an M-16, or any semi-automatic rifle, creates great heat which could damage the barrel. Castings from Jenkin's rifle were falling on Greg's back, giving him a burning sensation from the hot shell casings. That was likely the cause of Lt. King's rifle jamming. Greg was still near him and unable to fire his rifle due to his wounds, so he gave it to Dennis.

The bunker that was the source of the enemy fire was only 50 feet away. Greg could see that it had two firing ports, and two or three enemy soldiers were in it. Soon after the firefight began, the gunner (the soldier who carried an M-60 machine gun) came upfront and began firing his stream of hot lead.

After a while, Greg was able to crawl back to the area where Captain Wilson was positioned. They could see NVA soldiers dashing through the jungle at that location, but they disappeared in the heavy vegetation before they could kill them.

John Cirjak, the battalion RTO, remembers Jerry saying, "Where are they, where are they," as the bullets kept coming, and the source seemed invisible.

During a lull in the shooting, Cirjak was able to crawl back to where Doc, my platoon medic, was working on the wounded. He carried two wounded men back by placing them on his back as he crawled. When he thought he was at a safe distance, he would stand and carry them the rest of the way. That area had white medical gauze soaked with various amounts of blood spread all over the ground.

Doc was piecing the men together so they would be stable enough to be sent back to the rear on a medivac chopper. Similar to Luke 13:1, the blood of Bravo Company and the enemy mingled with the dirt below us.

When the shooting began, my platoon, and Guido's platoon, November, was behind Lima's platoon. My platoon was about 100 feet back, and November was about 200 feet back. However, by instinct, everyone dropped to the ground when we heard gunfire, not knowing how close the enemy might be. The cacophony of sounds from all the gunfire was deafening. I remember one GI near me who appeared to be frozen in place with his eyes in a glazed stare, staring with fear into nowhere. I was petrified but somehow functional. The fear permeated my whole being. It was a fear that I never knew existed. I prayed that my entire body would somehow merge with the earth beneath me, and I would become one with it and be encased by its security. Such a dream did not materialize.

We had encountered an undetermined number of regular North Vietnamese Army troops in a base camp. They were in multiple well-constructed bunkers.

Years later, my platoon medic, Ted, told me at a reunion of Bravo Company that he had always thought the October 2, 1969, battle took place on Halloween, over the years after returning to the US. It may have been because that holiday is one of evil spirits and death, describing what had happened to us that afternoon.

He said it felt like "we hiked into Hell that day." He further described his actions:

"When the bullets began flying, Sergeant Knowles jumped on top of me, looking scared to death. Leaving my position of relative security, I moved quickly towards the firefight. Little time passed before I was called to the front to take care of the wounded men of Lima and Mike platoons.

"Two GIs were dragging a soldier back to my position. Billy Renfro was a big guy who must have been over six feet in height. His size gave him the nickname of Mule. I had not seen any man fall from being shot, and I did not think he was severely wounded, so I began CPR, including mouth-to-mouth. As soon as I started, my mouth was filled with blood clots, causing me to vomit. Mule was dead.

"Other GIs needed my attention, and I went to help them. Captain Wilson's RTO called back, reporting that the CO had been hit. Bullets were flying everywhere and had sliced off the tops of bushes along the path I was crawling. I had done low crawling in basic training but never anything like this day. Fortunately, the CO's injury was a minor one on his scalp.

"Lt. Shannaussey, our forward observer, was hit. Another soldier and I crawled to him and dragged him back to a safer area. He had taken a direct hit to his leg from an RPG warhead that was a dud and therefore did not explode. He and anyone near him would have been in pieces and parts if it had.

"I helped wounded GIs go back to an area in a Rome Plow field that we used for medivac choppers to take away the wounded and the dead. That afternoon, the helicopter made continuous flights from the LZ to and from medical care facilities.

"My fatigues were soaked from head to toe with sweat, and I was physically and mentally exhausted from the terror we had seen and experienced. Night came, and I cried because so many had been killed or wounded from the battle, and we had not been ordered to pull back earlier."

I recall seeing Doc attempting to resuscitate Renfrow. When he realized that he could not, he sobbed tears of regret.

Two men in my platoon, Ron Farrow and Marshall Copeland, helped Doc drag Ron Hagstrom back from the front line. It was arduous since Ron was 6' 5" and weighed some 230 pounds. Navigating his body through the thick jungle growth was quite a challenge. When they got him back to a safer area, several other guys helped take him back to where the medivac chopper was coming in for the dead and wounded.

Jungle growth

Within a short time, the 1st platoon leader was wounded, and others in his platoon. The CO ordered Lt. Guido to take the third platoon to a position in the rear and secure a landing zone for the medivac choppers. I remember his "joy" when he had an assignment in the back. Remember, he already had six months in and was due for a staff job in the rear very soon.

Lt. Bill Guido in center

The firefight seemed to intensify. The battalion commander (Colonel Holt) was overhead in his Light Observation Helicopter (Loach), directing and coordinating our efforts. My CO called back on the radio, telling me to bring my platoon to the front. I had been expecting that order – and dreading its arrival.

Seconds before I received the call, a rocket darted across the sky and over our heads, exploding behind us. The NVA were now launching Rocket Propelled Grenades at us - not a good thing. When the CO called me forward, I said something like this over the radio: "We're getting RPGs back here." The CO responded, "I don't give a damn what you have back there; what the hell do you think we have up here – now get your ass up here." I simply replied, "Roger, Mike out." The

Battalion Commander in his Loach heard all this and said something like, "Now Capt. Wilson, keep your cool and stay focused." Colonel Holt knew that I was a new lieutenant. When I got to Captain Wilson, he apologized for his outburst. I told him to think nothing of it.

I collected my platoon and told them to move forward. The chaos and confusion of a firefight make any effort to coordinate most difficult. Besides, everyone was penetrated with near incapacitating fear. The noise from the exchange of bullets between the two armies was ferocious. It was a cacophony of hideous sounds. We heard the RAT, TAT, TAT, TAT, TAT repetition of the machine guns from both sides. The other semi-automatic rifles shook the airwaves. So many bullets came our way that they cut down the jungle growth about 18 to 24 inches from the ground. That jungle growth looked like it had received a haircut. Bullets were streaming everywhere.

I have found that my memory of what happened on October 2 is weak and scattered. The details are likely buried somewhere in the 85 billion neurons of my brain. Hopefully, they will not come to the surface. Others like Greg Drum, David Bowden, Ted Pettengill, and John Cirjak seem to have vivid memories of what happened. I suppose I have moved those memories to a deep storage place in my brain where they have not and may never come to the surface. That may be a great blessing.

David Bowden of my platoon is one who seemed to have retained his memories of that afternoon. In an email, he wrote:

> "We all moved online just as we were expected to do. They were passing in front and to the right of Capt. Wilson, Slim, and the rifle squad spread to the right. I stopped online about 25 yards in front of Capt. Wilson. To my left went Eddie Betzer, Beyman, and others. Beyman was about 25 to 30 feet from me, then Betzer was to his left and behind the M60. Beyman was holding the ammo belts to the gun as Betzer was shooting. To my right were Sim and the rifle squad. We all were firing our weapons. Bullets were going back and forth.

"An RPG round went over my head and Wilsons and exploded somewhere behind him. Someone yelled to pop purple smoke and throw it in front of us. I threw one and saw another one or two go in front, and then the smoke drifted back toward us. Bullets were streaming back and forth through the smoke when iron scraps suddenly fell from the sky like rain. I could see the rockets exploding behind us, just overhead and in front of us, just below the tops of the trees. I could hear the helicopters behind the missiles coming toward us. I stuck down to the ground and looked at Betzer and Beyman. They raised to look at the rocket exploding in the trees.

"Then, as fast as it started raining scraps of iron, it stopped. The helicopters passed, and all shooting stopped. I looked to the right and saw Slim and Chuck Snyder picking up guns and wounded and carrying them to the rear. I heard Betzer yell he had been hit. I could see Beyman was also hit. I told them to get back to the rear and get help, and I would take the gun. The shooting was still quiet for a short time when Hadley called me and asked if I would take the M60. I took over the gun and looked for the enemy.

Chuck Snyder at the base camp

"Hadley said Betzer had been shooting many bullets through the gun. I told him to get to my right and make sure we still had ammo linked together. Hadley cradled over me. Hadley said to shoot back at them. I answered, wait, something was going on in front of us. I could see movement about 25 to 30 yards in front of us. It came from a bunker with a machine gun in the front and a man behind loading another RPG to shoot at us.

"Just as they were setting into position, I fired and knocked the two out of the bunker. It was over. Slim and his rifle squad continued to carry the wounded back. I think Big Red came over and said we are moving back out of the jungle into a clear area to bring in more support. It was getting dark when we settled into a clear area outside the jungle then the jet came in to drop napalm. The next morning Delta Co. would come through and sweep the area toward us and access the damage. How long did this firefight last? I am not sure. But a lot of praying and bullets were fired on both sides. The Vietnamese were fighting for their country. We were fighting for our lives."[7]

---

[7] Email from David Bowden, October 15, 2012.

David Bowden – facing camera
Bob Gadd on right

My radio operator, Beaver, and I moved up to the right side of the line of Bravo Company. A Cobra gunship was circling overhead, waiting for instructions from the CO. Captain Wilson told me to pop a smoke grenade to mark our locations for the pilot. This was so he would know where we were located and not shoot us. Another soldier did the same on the left flank of our company. The two smoke grenade markers gave the pilot a picture of where we were in relation to the enemy. I pulled the pin on the smoke grenade and threw it in front of us. This was the first time I had thrown a smoke grenade in combat to mark our position. I was scared to death. Immediately after I threw the grenade, Beaver reprimanded me, who said that I threw the smoke grenade too close to our position. He had been with Bravo Company for at least eight months and knew the ins and outs. This turned out to be my first major mistake as a green lieutenant.

The Cobra was a devastating death machine, and it killed indiscriminately. The Cobra made multiple passes dispersing a wave of bullets parallel to our front line. When the Cobra fired its machine guns, it gave me a sense that we were in control of the situation. I knew the NVA did not have any choppers, and they could not match its firepower with rifles, machine guns, or RPGs. They would go where we needed them and made us feel more secure.

After returning home from Vietnam, my memory was that Beaver was wrong, and the gunship's firing was far enough from our men that no injuries occurred. No one had questioned my memory of this matter. It was not until late 2012 that I learned differently. Several times, I circulated an early draft of my battle account to men in my platoon, asking for their comments. One of my men, Chuck Snyder, emailed this to me:

> "You did not throw the smoke out far enough. You were not in front of the lead element. The smoke was actually behind Ed Betzer and his ammo bearer. Slim and I had just carried a wounded guy back, or we would have been up with Ed. I was not going to talk about this, but you keep bringing it up."

It was fortunate that I learned this after I had been in counseling for nearly two years. It might have been a devastating blow if I had become aware of it before counseling.

Lt. Tom McGrann sitting, Standing L to R, Sgt. Knowles, Glen Surrette (Slim)

I had been to Bravo Company reunions in 2004, 2006, and 2012 where Chuck and others in my platoon were present. No one ever referred to my mistake, including Ed Betzer. Without question, it was sobering information for me. I was brought to tears over 40 years later when I learned of it.

Throughout the afternoon, at least 18 men staggered to the rear to be medivaced out. Three soldiers died. I don't recall there being any prisoners. At least nine enemies were killed, and an unknown number escaped.

Late in the afternoon, Captain Wilson ordered the company to withdraw and set up for the night. We moved some 1,500 or 2,000 feet back from the battle area. We were in an open space for the night. The 3rd Platoon leader directed jets that dropped bombs on the target area during much of the night. There was also an AC-47, "Spooky" gunship operating. The loud buzz of the mini guns was a welcome sound. "In the beginning, the Douglas AC-47 was known as 'Puff the Magic Dragon,' in recognition of the amazing firepower it delivered to help troops in trouble. Eventually, it became known as a 'Spooky,' it's call sign in the country. The close air support that Spookies provided for beleaguered troops and remote FSBs out in the 'boonies' became legendary."[8]

From a 4,500-foot slant range, a four to five-second burst from just one gun would put 400 rounds within an impact area of 30 feet. The gunship was used in an attack on suspected Al-Qaeda members in Somalia on January 7, 2007. It had been improved since 1969:

> "The AC-130 gunship is a heavily armed aircraft, with four cannons and a six-barrel Gatling gun capable of firing 1,800 rounds a minute. But its most striking weapon is a computer-operated 105mm howitzer that juts sideways from the middle of the aircraft. An offensive behemoth that is relatively defenseless against counterattack, it is flown only at night."[9]

---

[8] Titus Lt. Col., Lowell, "GIs' Friendly Ghosts," *Vietnam*, August 2000, 38.
[9] IBID, 41.

Spooky was and is a formidable killing machine. We could see the tracers from its guns. The guns' roar and the tracer bullets' rapid stream made the sky appear like a blaze of fire.

We slept little, and the night was long and lonely. In a matter of a few hours, Bravo Company had shrunk from about 90 men to less than 70. The battle was a catastrophic event for all of us. I had over 11 months left in my one-year tour. The likelihood of me returning home alive or uninjured seemed to have diminished exponentially.

During one of my brief periods of sleep that night, I dreamed that choppers had come and taken everyone out but me. I was left alone next to the wood line marked by death. I was pleased to wake up and see that it was not so.

Sometime the following day, a fleet of Huey's did come and flew us back to the battalion base camp at Dau Tieng. We stayed there for five or six days. Usually, when we went to the base camp, it was for one day. However, we needed time to recover.

There was a memorial ceremony for the three that died. They were from the 1st platoon. The battalion commander let the ceremony. What was left of the 1st platoon stood at attention. In front of them were three rifles with bayonets stuck into the ground. On top of each rifle was a combat helmet, and there were three polished pairs of combat boots beside each rifle.

The only thing I remember the colonel saying is that they were "BRAVE SOLDIERS, BRAVE SOLDIERS." A few days later, we went back into the field. That was my worst day in Vietnam. At least I was no longer a green lieutenant. I had been baptized by fire and became a Casualty of War.

While I was in Vietnam, I sent several letters to my pastor and National Gardens Baptist Church members in northern Virginia. My first letter was sent on October 4, a few days after the encounter with the enemy. My pastor would post them on a bulletin board in the fellowship hall. Sylvia and my parents told me that many members read the letters. The first one included:

"There may be some of you who have the mistaken idea that I have a desk job and am in a relatively safe position. True, my education would logically place me in such a position, but the Army is not using me in such a capacity. I am in the jungle looking for the enemy with the mission to kill him. We do see the VC and NVA troops. They are the cold, blunt facts but the absolute truth. I say this to assure you that my men and I surely need your constant prayers. I have been very, very scared several times since arriving here. There is no way to express it in words."

I also wrote this: "Each of you, I'm sure, has somewhat different views of this war. But, believe me, if you are here with an M-16 in your hand out in the jungle, whatever reservations you might have had seem to vanish. Life and health become the ultimate concern."

In Vietnam, GIs used the one-liner term that captured the evaluation of the war as "don't mean nothing." They used it constantly in referring to most anything relating to the war. It was a phrase used to discount and ignore the terrible conditions we were forced to face. However, deep inside, we all knew that the horrors we faced meant EVERYTHING.

I told them: "There may have been times in your lives when you couldn't help but think that career military personnel were killers and maybe even enjoyed war. I can only think of a speech by General MacArthur to the 1961 graduating class at West Point when he said the soldier above all men hates war, for he must pay the greatest price."

In the October 4 letter, I wrote: "I will close with the thoughts of a professor of history at Bob Jones University, whom I greatly respect. He once asked the class if anything on earth could be worse than war. He answered himself by saying 'yes, tyranny and terror.' I believe he is right." Having experienced combat, I would add that war must always be the last resort and highlight that the professor had not experienced combat.

It was typical for soldiers in Vietnam to refer to things as wasted. That was the term used when one of our men was killed. The men may refer to him as "wasted." They did not know how true that would turn out to be. I concluded the letter: "I pray that somehow, someway, no more of your sons and loved ones need to come here and that my wife's and our future grandchildren never must bear arms against any man."

In one letter, I wrote: "I hope when you pray for me, you will be sure to remember the entire company. The team's effort is vital. Recently Bob Gadd, my radio operator, had some battery acid in his eyes, causing pain and discomfort. It was so bad that I called for a chopper to take him to the medical aid station at the base camp. When I told him a helicopter was coming for him, he said: 'But who will carry the lieutenant's radio?' He wasn't severely injured, but I felt that if he were dying, he would have the same reaction. This is the type of team effort that develops in a combat environment."

Batteries for our radios came wrapped in heavy plastic wrap. The wrap was used to cover the handset to our radios to keep them dry when it rained. The men kept photos and letters in them for the same reason. I usually had three radios in the platoon. I had one with me, the platoon sergeant had one, and there was one at the rear of our column.

I also sent Sylvia a four-page letter on October 4. What was I to tell her about the battle? I expected it would have been on the national news and identified the unit as the First Infantry Division and may have included that it was my battalion. A reporter would likely have said that there was a battle northwest of Saigon. I told her that our base camp was 45 miles from Saigon. This is what I wrote:

"We had a little shooting on Thursday the 2nd. I saw some of it, but it was over pretty quickly. I even got to fire my rifle. It shoots well; however, I never did see a target, just trees, and bushes." That was the truth, although it was not the whole truth and nothing but the truth.

Late in September, I picked up a head cold which was a problem. I got some medication for it, and it seemed to be about over early in early October.

In an October 5 letter, I told Sylvia that I had read Psalms 46 that day. Considering the October 2 battle, I expect I was concentrating on verse 1: "God is our refuge and strength, a very present help in trouble."

October 7 was a "red letter" day since I received seven letters at the mail call. Four were from Sylvia, one from her parents, one from my parents, and one from my brother, Paul. It would take six or seven days for letters to get to me from the States. Since we were in the jungle, we only got mail every three days and they could pile up at the base camp.

During the summer of 1969, President Nixon announced that he was initiating a program to turn the fighting over to the South Vietnamese. The program was called "Vietnamization." As I was arriving on September 1, 25,000 were coming home. Actually, fewer GIs went to Vietnam instead of anyone coming home, and units began withdrawing. In April 1970, a firebase operated by the South Vietnamese was overrun by the Viet Cong soldiers. They killed the guards and planted satchel charges throughout the base, destroying artillery and bunkers. In a letter to Sylvia, I wrote: "This is the type of thing that makes the effectiveness of Vietnamization suspect.

8

The Lieutenants Dilemma

"I hate war and love the warriors."
- Leon Standifer, author of *Not in Vain,* WWII veteran

In *The Patriot,* Mel Gibson plays a planter in South Carolina during the Revolutionary War. He wants freedom from Britain and supports the patriots but he cannot go to war with Britain. He exhibits pacifist qualities since he would not join the freedom fighters. His oldest son rebels and joins the Continental army. Later, when his son is home on leave from the war, a British unit attacks his farmhouse, burns it, captures his son, and kills his next oldest son, a teen. Gibson is outraged and has a change of heart.

After the soldiers leave with his oldest son as a prisoner, he has his two youngest sons join him and seek out his son's killers. The three are in the woods at the top of a gulley with a dirt road below. The unit that killed his son is approaching.

He asks the boys whether they know how to identify the officers. They replied that they do. He instructs them when they shoot: "I want you boys to start with the officers and work your way down."

That was the dilemma any infantry leader faced in South Vietnam, whether a sergeant, company commander, or lieutenant. It was common knowledge among OCS candidates of the risks a lieutenant faced in combat. There were various claims that second lieutenants lasted only a short time in a firefight. Ron Milam, Ph.D., in *Not a Gentleman's War: An Inside View of Junior Officers in the Vietnam War*, wrote:

> "The commonly held belief and Hollywood-inspired belief that the average life span of an infantry lieutenant was minutes was probably an exaggerated claim, but the danger for lieutenants exceeded that of other ranks."[10]

This knowledge raised my distaste for the US Army recruiters who misled me.

I was usually towards the front of a column moving through the jungle. I was the second or third man in my queue. The man closest to me would always be my RTO. He carried his radio on his back, and the antenna pointing into the sky was like a giant arrow over our heads with large letters on it reading "kill them first."

I expect this is what happened on Halloween evening in 1969. The CO would have had two RTOs, one radio for communicating with his three platoons and the other to communicate with battalion headquarters on a separate frequency. The whip antenna for the battalion radio was significantly longer than the company radio and, therefore, more visible. On that occasion, Captain Saunders was the only person wounded.

From time to time, as we were moving through the jungle or taking a rest, the thought would come to mind that a VC sniper might be in the trees near me with the crosshairs of his scope fixed on my helmet or the heart of the guy next to the soldier carrying the radio.

Another element of the lieutenant's dilemma was that I was responsible for the lives of some 30 men in my platoon. I made daily decisions that would affect their safety and security. We were trained well in OCS; however, my ultimate responsibility was in South Vietnam. It required that EVERY decision I made had to be the right one. I was not satisfied that 90% of them were the right ones – it had to be 100%. Otherwise, someone could be injured or worse. Of course, it

---

[10] Ron Milam, *Not a Gentlemen's War*, (The University of North Carolina Press), 4.

was not possible to be correct all the time. Add to that the stress of a combat environment and mistakes are bound to be made. In effect, infantry platoon leaders and company commanders were "set up" to fail because we would not and could not always be perfect.

In an April 2 letter to the church members, I wrote:

"I'm sure you've heard and read about the troops' high use of marijuana (pot or grass). My experience has been that not as many used it as reported in the States. Anyone in my platoon that I could prove was using it would meet the most severe punishment I could have a court-martial board administer judgment My reason would be that he would be endangering everyone else due to his reduced awareness of his surroundings. In a firefight, this would be disastrous."

No landline telephones were available for soldiers or sailors to call family members back home during the Vietnam conflict. To address this, United States MARS (*Military Affiliate Radio Service*) stations from all service branches, Army, Navy, Marines, and Air Force, were deployed throughout Vietnam. The MARS system offered soldiers and sailors a way to personally communicate with loved ones back home via a "phone-patch" telephone connection over short-wave radio. MARS stations would allow each soldier a 5-minute personal call home to the United States. When making calls, I needed to remember that there was a half-day difference in times. In almost all cases, MARS was the only way soldiers could call home. In other words, "MARS was the soldiers' Telephone Company."

In early October, I made my first MARS call to Sylvia. I would go to the MARS station at the battalion base camp, sign up to make a call, and then come back to the station when they expected to make the connection. The connection would be made to a short-wave operator in the States who would connect it to the phone lines of the person receiving the call. Since it was a short-wave radio setup, the callers would have to say "over" when they were finished. That way, the person on the other end would know it was their turn to talk. It was awkward for Sylvia initially, but she caught on to it quickly. The cost of the call was one dollar.

Several of the company's men had cassette tape recorders that were used to send and receive tape letters home. In an October 5 letter to Sylvia, I suggested she purchase two small cassette tape recorders to exchange tapes. Soon after, she sent me a recorder, and we began exchanging tape letters. It was a great way to communicate, considering the distance between us. It almost made it seem like we were in the same room, talking to each other.

We went on a mission looking for a weapons cache that a VC deserter told us about one day. It turned out to be empty. He had seen it nine months before.

I kept photos that Sylvia sent me in a plastic bag inside the liner of my steel helmet to keep them dry. I also used the steel helmet to hold water while I shaved each morning. In a letter to Sylvia, I wrote: "You know, I believe my morale is higher when we are in the field than at the base camp. I have too much free time when we return to Dau Tieng."

When I left for Vietnam, there was much discussion about building a subway in the Washington, DC area. Before leaving, I had written a letter to *The Washington Post*'s editor, encouraging it to build it. Sylvia sent me various new clippings indicating that construction had begun, so I told her not to send the letter. My penchant for letter writing to newspapers was stopped for a time.

On Thursday, October 9, Mike and Lima Platoons went to the airstrip to be airlifted to an area to look for another enemy weapon cache. It turned out that 50 Armed Forces Vietnam (ARVN) soldiers were also going, and there was not enough room for my platoon, so we returned to the Company area. It seemed that someone at the battalion in the S-3 office should have known about this and saved us the trip.

Delta Company found an underground VC/NVA medical station in early October. I saw the equipment they brought back – all kinds of pills, bandages, and other medical paraphernalia. It looked like it came from a hospital.

One evening, around 8 pm, we heard movement to the rear of our ambush. The sound moved from our left to right. I took out my starlight scope to look around and saw no one walking around. We heard the noise again a half-hour later, and it sounded closer to our position than earlier. I took no chances and flipped my M-16 to automatic since the sound was coming right at me. I told the guys in our ambush not to fire because I thought it was an animal. Soon I sensed a foul odor, which turned out to be three or four wild hogs. They scampered through our ambush and were on their way. Shortly after that, I recorded on my tape diary that life in the field made me "kind of edgy." In another tape, I said, "If I am careful, and I am. If I know what I'm doing, and I do, I will be fine."

One night I awoke and realized that a snake was crawling across my ankles from right to left. I could tell that it was a pretty good size snake. Since it was moving across both ankles and not towards my face, I decided to do nothing and hoped it went on its way. It did.

On October 15, a "Peace Moratorium" took place in the US. An estimated two million people participated, with about 250,000 demonstrators gathering in Washington, DC. Senator Edward Kennedy called for combat troops to be withdrawn by the end of 1972. He added, "I do believe this nation is in danger of committing itself to goals and personalities that guarantee the war's continuance."[11]

At that time, my view of the war was documented in a letter to Sylvia: "I think maybe the protest on October 15 was in the wrong direction. Why not protest the efforts of Hanoi? What more should we do – lay down our arms and greet the VC with gifts? A little pressure on Hanoi to take their troops home is what we need. Nixon may have been right when he called Vietnam 'America's finest hour.' Somewhere behind the smoke, the thousands killed, everyone here has seen a glimpse of light that shines brightly on a politically free nation. Enough of the right people have seen that the results of this war will set the pace of advance for the Communist World."

In the following years, my views altered significantly as I became more aware and had a fuller and more informed understanding of Vietnam's situation.

---

[11] http://news.bbc.co.uk/onthisday/hi/dates/stories/october/15/newsid_2533000/2533131.stm

On October 11, we were airlifted to an LZ and moved northward, checking out an ARC light (an area where B-52s put in an airstrike) the previous night. Operation Arc Light was when B-52s from Anderson Air Force Base in Guam, 2,600 miles away, were deployed to South Vietnam on bombing missions. The bombers could carry 60,000 pounds of bombs. They would release their 500- and 750-pound bombs from the stratosphere. Each bomb would create a crater 15 feet deep and 30 feet wide. When the bombs exploded, we could feel the earth vibrate under our feet, and we heard a distinct rumbling sound. It was a scary experience since we hoped they would not drop their payload too close to us.

While I was in Vietnam, I understood that a single Arc Light strike would cost millions of dollars. In a tape to Sylvia, I said: "I don't care. I will pay it because one GI is worth 30 million dollars as far as I am concerned."

On Monday afternoon, October 13, the company had been in a blocking force since 1:00 p.m. At about 4:15 p.m., the CO radioed me to get ready to move in five minutes: we were going to a "Pick up Zone" (PZ) and taken to another LZ. We managed to get to the PZ and were finally picked up at 6:30 p.m. By the time the entire company arrived, it was 7:30 p.m. and dark. A "Snoopy" gunship was dropping flares all around for A Company, which had been air lifted earlier. Our LZ was wet with about an inch of water, and it began to rain. In addition, we were told that 30 VCs were moving toward us. We had all our guns in position and were ready for them. We never saw any VC. We stayed until 10:30 p.m. and were instructed to move into the wood line and set up a perimeter. Have you ever tried to do that in the dark? We finally managed to accomplish the feat. We were wet and cold all night. The noise of "Snoopy" hosing down an area with miniguns nearby kept us awake most of the night. On top of that, artillery was firing all night and jet fighters struck with their bombs within miles of our location.

In an October 14 letter to Sylvia, I wrote, "Today we have been checking the area for bomb damage, VC, etc. We found nothing except holes in the ground. We are now in positions for the night and will be air lifted tomorrow afternoon somewhere else in this land of opportunity."

On one occasion, Bravo Company received a mission to rescue a spotter plane pilot shot down near the Cambodian border. We air assaulted the area only to learn that another unit had already saved him.

Our new mission was to check out the area for enemy activity. While doing that, we came upon some shallow grave of a dead VC. The only remains were bleached white bones and what remained of his black PJs. The stench was terrible. Bob Gadd, my RTO, recalls that: "We also found five or six more graves nearby where one was a woman because her long hair was sticking out of the shallow grave."

We were near the Cambodian border and stayed there for several more days to find the enemy. Sometime during these discoveries, I was brought to tears at the horrible spectacles. Bob tried to comfort me by saying that these are the fortunes of war, and we have to deal with the good and the bad.

Sometimes we needed to clear an area to make an LZ. That would be accomplished with machetes, Claymore mines, and pure muscle.

When General Westmorland was commander, he came up with the idea of teaching a "crossover" point. That would be the point where we were able to kill more enemy soldiers than North Vietnam was able to replace. That policy put a premium on killing Vietnamese soldiers. On several occasions, I had some of my men be awarded for direct kills. They got a three-day pass to Vung Tau, the in-country R&R location.

Reaching that crossover point would have required more troops than we ever committed to Vietnam. The peak troop strength was 543,400 in the spring of 1969. A history professor at the University of Vermont wrote this to me:

> "The figure I have previously heard and usually cite regarding the number of troops necessary to 'win' in Vietnam is two million. I first heard that figure when I spent a year in the Strategy Department of the Naval War College in the early 1980s. I have since heard it repeated but could not give you a specific citation. Of course, it is no more than an educated guess, but I believe it is based on the number of troops

North Vietnam could replace annually as well as the extensive US logistical tale."

During one period of time the platoon only had about 15 men due to GI's rotating home. David Bowden got a nasty insect bite on his lip. It was painful but with no other side effects. He asked if I would call a chopper to take him into the base camp for treatment and a break. David carried one of our machine guns which was an important part of our arsenal.

I told him that because we were so low and that he was not having a severe reaction I could not let him go. He did not say anything but if looks could kill, I would have fallen over dead. After returning home I have seen him at reunions. He has told me that he is glad that I was his platoon leader.

A Claymore mine was a portable bomb with a 100-foot electric wire from the mine back to a soldier. Detonating the mine required the soldier to squeeze the firing mechanism (called a clacker since it made a clacking sound when depressed), which would generate an electrical charge that would set off the firing detonator and the mine. The mine had a front and back, with the front facing where the enemy would be located. The front side was marked with this warning, "This Side Towards Enemy." If it were reversed, the GIs would be killing themselves upon detonation. I would have someone check each Claymore after it was set up to ensure it was facing the enemy. This was more important if we were in an area where we thought the danger level was unusually high. The men (and I) would be particularly nervous and could easily screw up and have the Claymore facing us by mistake. We were in a place and environment where errors had to be minimized. The goal was to eliminate them, but we were human, although sometimes we may have wondered about that.

The Claymore was an effective weapon. When it was detonated, 8,000 steel pellets flew out to the front. They would go at high speed for 150 meters in a burst of up to 100 feet in width. Anyone or anything on the receiving end would be perforated with steel pellets. In a 2009 email Bob Brown, one of my men, described a Claymore ambushes this way:

"A Claymore ambush was set up using one or more Claymore anti-personal mines. Normally, the Claymore was hand detonated using a hand detonator (called a 'clacker' because of the clacking sound when pressed) connected to the Claymore using a lamp cord ('clacker wire') looking wire with a blasting cap on one end and a plug for the 'clacker' on the other.

"To set up a Claymore ambush, we split the 'clacker wire' partway and cut one of the two wires. The cut wire was stripped on both sides of the cut. We then wrapped the wire around a thumbtack and pushed the thumbtack into a spring-type wooden clothespin our parents sent us back in the World. A piece of plastic was tied to a tripwire and inserted between thumbtacks. The other end of the tripwire was strung across the trail, road, or area we were ambushing. The plug was cut off the end of the 'clacker wire.' The wire was stripped and connected to a battery.

"The battery was carried by the person setting up the ambush to prevent someone from connecting it and setting the Claymore off."

After the Claymores were out and everything was set, each of us would pick his favorite place on the ground to sleep and have dinner. We called it a night at about 8 pm, which under the jungle canopy, was when it was getting dark. Each AP had someone on guard all night. A time at guard would be about an hour, so each man usually had guard twice each night. I pulled guard along with everyone else in the AP since rank was irrelevant regarding guard duty. We had a poncho liner to keep out mosquitoes and keep us warm during the night when the temperature dropped.

Generally, a platoon met with three to 10 enemies at a time. They were usually immensely outnumbered, and when contact was made, the CO called for a gunship or armed aircraft over us. Artillery was always available and used at an instant's notice. Even if it was just one VC armed with a rifle, massive firepower was placed upon him and where he was expected to escape. Usually, their minutes were numbered when we clashed with them unless they could run. Prisoners were not traditionally taken because a GI would fire everything he had. This usually eliminated the possibility of any enemy coming out alive.

All in all medically we were in pretty good hands. A Red Cross evacuation helicopter could be overhead in 10 minutes or less in an emergency. If a man is hurt, every human effort is immediately made to give him medical attention. What is reported in the states about medical attention being swift is true. I don't know what Charlie has to look to when wounded. There are no helicopters for him and very little of anything.

One evening around 11 pm, while we were at the base camp, the company executive officer woke me and told me that my platoon was to eat breakfast at 5:30 am. I was to go to the TOC at 6 am for instructions about taking the platoon out of the defensive perimeter to see whether artillery killed any VC spotted on the radar that evening. We accomplished this and were ready to leave the east gate at 6:26 am. I made a communication check with the TOC at 6:30 to ensure everything was set for us to proceed. A TOC (Tactical Operations Center) is a command post for the battalion. It consists of a small group of officers and enlisted personnel who guide the battalion elements during a mission.

I was advised to wait before departing. In about one minute, the duty officer called back, informing me that the mission was canceled and trucks were on the way to bring us back to the company area.

The original plan for the company that morning was to go to the firing range and test fire our rifles and machine guns. It was always a wise idea to ensure your weapon was correctly fired. The rest of the company met us at the gate at 7:30, and we were off to the range. However, at about 7:35, Captain Wilson called me on the radio and said he was returning to my position. The initial mission was back on, and we were to return to the east gate at 7:45 and complete the task. Such was the inconstancy and continuously changing nature of war. I guess this was part of the training in OCS when we were thrown new circumstances or instructions in an instant and expected to adjust – "RIGHT NOW," not in 10 minutes.

Our new CO was Captain Saunders. He was married and had one child; his last station was in Denver. Captain Wilson went out into the field for seven days to teach him the "ropes" of being a company commander. Captain Wilson went back to the states around the third week of October when his one-year tour ended.

After about a month as a platoon leader, I wrote Sylvia, "I'm pretty well into the swing of how things go now. When something comes up, I usually know what to do or where to go. It has not been quite as difficult as I had expected." This was a case where I did not tell the "whole truth" and nothing but the truth. I am sure she saw through my claim.

Bravo Company set up as a blocking force on one operation at 1:00 pm. Three hours later, Captain Saunders radioed me and said to be ready to move out in five minutes. We were to proceed to a pick-up zone and be extracted out to a landing zone. We arrived at the PZ but were not picked up until 6:30 pm. When the rest of the company arrived, it was 7:30 and dark. A Snoopy gunship was dropping flares in the area for Alpha Company, which had airlifted earlier. The LZ was wet with about an inch of water everywhere, and it began to rain. We were told that 30 VC was moving towards our location. We were ready for them. We stayed there until 10:30 pm. There had been no sign of any enemy movement, so we were instructed to move further into the jungle and set up a perimeter for the night. The only worse thing than tromping through the jungle is to do it at night. We accomplished the task with considerable difficulty and complaining from the troops. We were wet and cold another night.

Half the night, a Snoopy gunship was hosing down the area with its mini-guns. In addition, artillery dropped in 105 mm rounds where the VC were thought to be located. Not far away, jets were conducting airstrikes. With all that noise and confusion, none of us got much sleep.

On Saturday, October 11, we were airlifted to an LZ close to where a B-52 Arc Light strike had taken place. We traversed swamps and chest-deep streams to get to the location. We were wet, muddy, miserable, and tired when we got to the correct site. We were to search the area of the bomb strike and report our findings. We found a couple of bunkers, and Alpha Company found over 20 bunkers, all of which were empty. A firefight was avoided.

A few days later, we were scheduled for a resupply, which would include clean uniforms. I was ready for them because my pants had split in the rear two days earlier.

In October, the company received two new medics. Our platoon medic, Ted Pettengill (Doc), was assigned to the company commander's Command element, so I received one of the new ones. Everyone in the platoon was sorry to see Doc leave us.

Next to the United States, South Korea had the most troops in South Vietnam. They had 350,000 soldiers fighting there, Thailand committed nearly 50,000 soldiers and sailors to the cause, and Australia had some 60,000 involved. China and the Soviet Union played significant roles in supporting their communist ally. Russia supplied arms, and more than 320,000 Chinese troops assisted the North Vietnamese between 1965 and 1971.

My experience with the Australian troops was with their pilots of observation aircraft. The aircraft often used was the Cessna O-2 Skymaster. They flew observation missions to search out an area and report back to a jet or gunship pilot. They would then "take out" the target. Often one would appear in our area and make radio contact with the CO.

He would throw out a smoke grenade (usually yellow) to show the pilot where we were located. He would reply, "I see Yankee smoke," to confirm that he knew our location. Sometimes he would kid us by pointing out that he was up in the air flying, and we were on the ground, and he would be going back to get hot meals and have a roof over his head.

We communicated with each other via radio. Each unit had a unique call sign. The call sign for our battalion was Dracula. The call signs for the companies within the battalion were Alpha, Bravo, Charlie, and Delta. In each case, the person "in charge" would add the number 6 to the call sign. So, the battalion commander was Dracula 6 or "Drac" 6, and our company commander was Bravo 6. Since I was in Mike platoon, I was Mike 6. A conversation between our company commander and the Aussie pilot would go something like this:

Aussie - "Bravo 6, this is Dragon 3, over. What are you guys up to today, it's a great view up here, but we all should be at the beach in California?"

CO -"Roger that, but we are all stuck here."

Aussie - Which direction are you heading ? Pop a smoke."

The CO would now have someone throw out a smoke grenade to show the pilot our position.

CO - Smoke out, over."

Aussie -"I see Yankee (yellow) smoke, over."

CO -"Roger, Yankee smoke, over."

The CO would not identify the color of the smoke in advance; he would wait for the pilot to say the color so he knew it was the pilot and not a VC speaking. Yankee meant yellow smoke.

CO - We are heading north searching for some reported bunkers; how about taking a fly up there and tell us what you see, over."

Aussie -"Roger, will do, out."

Ten minutes later, the pilot comes back online.

Aussie -"You are half a click from a large steam and very heavy vegetation ; I do not see any bunkers or enemy activity. It looks like you are smooth sailing, over."

CO - Roger, thanks; see you tomorrow, Bravo 6 out."

When the company or a platoon had a jet fighter overhead on a bombing mission, the Aussie pilot would direct the jet pilot. The Aussie fixed-wing aircraft was very maneuverable, and he could fly low and see the target area. He would lead the jet pilot to the target. If the first bomb was off the mark, he might tell him, "You need to strike 25 meters further northwest," and the jet pilot would comply and get right on target. The Aussie got what we needed where we needed it.

Jet bombers and artillery strikes were a lifesaver for the grunts on the ground. The jets could put down 250, 500, 750, or 1,000 bombs to "soften up the area." The Cobra Gunship was one of the best "security blankets" for us. They would go anywhere and put down a barrage of bullets and rockets. Their tremendous firepower made us feel a bit more secure.

My time experiencing combat was an unwanted opportunity to learn various things. One thing that became crystal clear to me was that "there are no winners in war; only varying degrees of losers."

Soldier who replaced Ted Pettengill as Doc

Taking a break after a long, tiring day

9

Time on Target

"We didn't know who we were till we got there. We thought we were something else."

- Robert Stone, *Dog Soldiers*

Troops in Vietnam got around by foot, tanks, armored personnel carriers, and helicopters. The helicopter is the mode I remember most vividly, and it was used most of the time. If we were going into an area, we would be heading for a Landing Zone (LZ). This was called an "insertion." Choppers were our taxi. If we were being picked up from a field in the jungle, we would be taken out of a Pickup Zone (PZ). It was called an "extraction." When we were being inserted into an LZ, we would be participating in an "air assault." An assault by helicopters was called an "Eagle Flight."

A well-executed air assault or extraction was a work of art. Proper execution of both was of such importance that on January 9, 1970, the battalion commander issued a nine-page "Letter of Instruction, Air Assaults." It read, "This letter has been compiled after a study of 75 air assaults conducted by the 1st Bn, 2nd Inf, during August-December 1969. These procedures standardize techniques between air mission commanders, battalion operations officer, and battalion and company commanders. They are detailed at battalion level, yet are general at company level to provide optimal uniformity while allowing maximum initiative by ground commanders."

Often, we would be extracted from the airstrip at Dau Tieng for a combat air assault. Trucks would bring us out to the airstrip from our company area. If the helicopters were not already at the airstrip, we would wait for them in the hot sun (we went out on UH-1 choppers, which were called Huey's). Six of us would board one Huey, and the rest of the platoon would get on one of the other four ships. The five ships were referred to as a "lift," and one would deliver a platoon to the LZ, thus requiring three lifts to transport a company. The ships were in a formation of three on one side and two on the other. Usually, the first lift would be waiting on the tarmac of the Dau Tieng airstrip for some time. It was probably 10 or 15 minutes but seemed like hours to us. It was stressful because we never knew whether we would be going into a hot LZ. I cannot explain the feeling as we approached the ground and the machine guns on the ship were blasting away. Many thoughts ran through my mind. I would glance at the other men on the chopper and wonder what they were thinking. The noise of the engine and rotor blades did not make it conducive for conversation, so we were alone with our thoughts as the blades spun overhead. Once the first lift reached the LZ, they would return to the airstrip to pick up another lift until the entire company was inserted into the LZ.

Bravo Company on the tarmac waiting for choppers

The first lift would see the LZ being "prepped" since it would be at an altitude of about 3,000 feet. Prepped meant howitzer artillery pieces would fire 105 mm artillery shells into and around the LZ to destroy potential enemy threats. In artillery terms, this was a Time on Target (TOT) tactic, "...a surprise tactic for devastating a particular target area almost instantaneously. Suspected 'hot' LZs were often prepared with a TOT mission while the assault forces hovered or circled overhead at altitude. Troops were then inserted into the 'sanitized' LZ before the smoke cleared."[12] Clearly, a TOT mission was an effective tactic.

TOT missions involved timing the firing of multiple batteries so that all fire on the exact location, with the firing times adjusted to cause the rounds to all impact simultaneously. A typical TOT might involve four batteries (24 guns) of different calibers: some firing shells fused for ground bursts, some for airbursts. The effect is that a particular jungle clearing might be quiet and peaceful one second and be enveloped and saturated with explosions in the air and on the ground in the next second. Bombardment may cease after the initial volley or be maintained in Fire for Effect mode, creating a sustained area saturated with detonations.[13]

The concept of "a particular jungle clearing might be quiet and peaceful one second and a barrage of explosions the next" was well presented in the film *We Were Soldiers* when Lt. Col. Hal Moore's battalion is inserted into the Ia Drang Valley in mid-November 1965. The camera shows tranquil shots in an open area, and then it turns to chaos instantly. They could have improved the effect by including the eerie whistling sounds of the 105 rounds coming into the area. We would hear that distinct sound when we called for artillery, and the location of the FSB was such that the shots came nearly overhead or to the left or right of us. Artillery did not fire rounds directly over a friendly unit because of the possibility of short rounds, which was when a round fell short of the target. If that happened, we would be in the line of fire.

---

[12] Mike Hopkins, http://www.vietvet.org/arty.htm
[13] Ibid.

From an altitude of about 3,000 feet, we could see the rounds exploding on the ground. This bombardment would continue for 12 minutes. The shells had a bursting radius of 150 to 200 feet, and the LZ was saturated with the barrage of chunks of hot metal speeding through the air. On one of the tapes, I said the explosions were "... a good sight to see that stuff coming in because you knew it would clear out (kill) anyone in the area."

While the LZ was being prepped, two Cobra helicopter gunships would be flying in the area, waiting for the moment they would perform their part in the assault. After the artillery prep was completed, the operations officer for the air assault gave the "go signal" for the two gunships to make their passes. One on each of the two sides of the LZ would swoop in with his armaments firing. They had mini-guns firing 3,000 rounds per minute, each with 10 2.75-inch rockets. They made two passes unleashing their deadly ordinance. Thirty seconds to one minute before the first lift landed, the gunships made a final pass buzzing over the area, firing their mini-guns and rockets to destroy any remaining aggressors.

As the first lift came into the LZ, the door gunner on the chopper would fire his machine gun into the wood line, and anywhere he suspected trouble. On one insertion, I recall the pilot signaled the gunner behind him (and in front of me) to direct his fire more to the front of the chopper. He immediately swung his machine gun from firing to the side of the ship to the front. The pilot seemed pleased to see the tracers going into the wood line to the front of the ship. The stream of tracers looked like a red waterfall shooting into the jungle growth. I wondered what the pilot saw and was more uneasy about the mission than usual.

The ships often did not always completely touch down on the LZ. They would hover two feet above the ground, and the grunts would jump off. Immediately after the last soldier was off, the ships would rise quickly into the sky as they arced to the right or left out of the line of fire of any enemy soldiers. We would promptly rush to the wood line so we would not be as vulnerable in the open field. I had told the platoon sergeant and squad leaders where each should take the men so everyone knew where to go upon their boots touching the ground. It was important for everyone to go to the right place and to do it fast since one could never be sure if Charlie might still be there.

The Officer in Charge of the landing of the first lift was to report to the battalion and company commander immediately, either "Lima Zulu Hot" or "Lima Zulu Cold." Hot meant the enemy was firing at you, and cold meant that there were not there. He would also "pop" a smoke grenade to mark the other lifts' spot to aim for when they landed.

If I was not on the first ship, I could hear the officer on the first ship report on the radio whether the LZ was hot or cold. We were joyful when we heard "Lima Zulu Cold." Captain Wilson was always on the first and last ship out. He had been a platoon leader earlier and knew how stressful it was for the officer who hit a "hot" LZ. He wanted to lessen the pressure on the platoon leaders. I do not recall whether my subsequent company commanders followed that policy.

I remember once when I was on the first lift, so I would report to the S-3 whether the LZ was cold or hot. The LZ was cold, and I went to pop the smoke for the next lift. I was nervous, and somehow, I got the smoke grenade in the wrong position, and when I pulled the pin, the smoke exhaust end was pointed towards my hand instead of away from it. I got a nasty burn from that mistake.

One of my greatest fears was to hit a hot LZ because we would be exposed and vulnerable in the open field. I do not recall that we did, and none of my letters or tapes refers to landing in a hot LZ.

The ordeal of a combat air assault insertion was an elating and intensely frightening experience. I never got used to them, and I participated in many. Air assaults and extractions were complex activities requiring coordination, planning, checking and rechecking, and supervision. In ways, it was amazing that anyone could pull them off.

Soon after arriving at Dau Tieng, I sent Sylvia a copy of our map on operations. In a letter, I tried to explain how to read it and determine where I was when I gave her the coordinates of places we searched in a previous operation.

Captain Wilson went home in early November. Captain Saunders replaced him.

In 1966 St. John F. Baker earned the Metal of Honor for actions he performed under fire near Dau Tieng. He is credited with recovering eight fallen US soldiers, destroying six bunkers, and killing 10 enemies. During the remainder of his tour, he was a tunnel rat. A tunnel rat would usually be a short and small soldier who could fit into the VC tunnels. He would be armed with a flashlight and a pistol and explore the underground network created by and used by the VC guerillas. It would not be unusual to find full-scale hospitals underground with surgical suites three stories below ground.

The VC built an extensive mass of tunnels throughout South Vietnam. They began construction in the 1940s when the French were in the country.

In October, I began a system of fines for people who fell asleep on guard. Depending on rank, it ranged from $15 to $75 for the first offense. A second offense ranged from $30 to $100. When we went to the base camp for a break, the money was used to buy sodas, food, beer, writing paper, and other items for the platoon. I collected the money on payday.

The protests against the war in the States substantially impacted my brother, Paul, who was attending Virginia Polytechnic Institute in Blacksburg, Virginia. He was a Cadet Lt. Colonel Battalion Commander in the Corps of Cadets at Virginia Tech. He sent me a paper that read, "On this day, October 15, 1969, as well as every day, WE, the members of L Company VTCC, support MIKE PLATOON and every US Serviceman in Vietnam." One hundred and sixty-one cadets signed it.

"Back in the World," October 15 was Moratorium Day (M-Day). Nationwide over a million people expressed their displeasure with the war in Vietnam. Over 250,000 protestors took to the streets in New York City. There were 200,000 in Boston, and a candlelight parade of 50,000 filed past the White House in Washington, DC. The widow of Dr. Martin Luther King led the procession.

On November 3, President Nixon addressed the nation about the war. He also extended his domino theory to the rest of the World by predicting that if the United States pulled out of Vietnam too fast, it would spark violence wherever our commitments help maintain the peace anywhere in the Western Hemisphere. Eisenhower's invalid domino theory remained alive and well.

Bravo Company was set up as a blocking force in early November while Delta Company was searching a bunker complex to our north. If there should be any VC or NVA in the bunkers and they tried to escape to the south, we'd get them! It looked like they were not around, though. Five days before, we went through the same area and found fresh rice, medical supplies, and explosives. The bunkers were only two weeks old.

It seemed that everyone wanted to get a poncho, flashlight, money, or something from a VC that had been killed or from a base camp that they left in a hurry. The guys wanted me to take some VC money from the stuff we found, but somehow, I didn't want anything from anyone over there, especially from a VC that had been killed, and especially if I knew I had killed him. I'd have plenty of vivid memories for souvenirs, and some of those I wished could be erased. But I guess such has been one of the many high costs of war through the ages.

In a November 5 letter to my pastor and church members, I wrote: "Here is a little more insight into what it is like over here. I'll never be able to explain what it's like entirely. I can't explain what fear feels like when you and Charlie meet. You'll have to see a dead VC to know what it's like. I can't explain the anxiety of being the first helicopter lift into a landing zone with their machine guns blasting away."

The largest anti-war demonstration ever held in Washington, DC, occurred during November 13-15. Two hundred and fifty thousand people attended the three-day protest, and another 200,000 demonstrated in other parts of the country. Those demonstrations did not affect the everyday lives of the grunt on the ground. We went about our daily routine of looking for Charlie with the intent to kill him if he showed his face.

On October 16, the company was running low on water, so the battalion sent out a water trailer with 100 gallons of water by chopper. We made Kool-Aid with the excess. The company learned about going to the base camp on October 17. We set up a Night Defensive Position (NDP) perimeter, and everyone in my platoon was so excited that we would be going into the base camp the following day that we could not sleep. I slept less than five hours. It was almost like Christmas Eve for a six-year-old.

We went into the base camp on October 18, and my platoon served as a ready reaction force in case the battalion needed more troops somewhere fast. Lima platoon took it over the following day. We thought we would have to go out this afternoon on a mission but another battalion took care of it.

Sylvia sent me frequent "care" packages with goodies. The platoon guys loved for me to get them because I would share with them. My platoon sergeant, "Pops," said she made some excellent chow. She would send eight-ounce cans of corn, lima beans, spaghetti, chili, fruits, juice, and homemade cookies. One of Sylvia's care packages was a photo that accented her beauty. When I saw it, I said aloud: "My Heavens, what am I doing here!"

On one of the tapes, I said I was smoking a cigar now and then. It seems that I smoked one about once a week, and at one point, I stopped for two weeks to ensure I was not getting hooked on them. I found that I was not. I said I did not smoke cigarettes because I did not want to get addicted to them. Oh yes, regarding the cigars, I did not inhale!

When we were at Dau Tieng on stand down, the CO and others would go to the Officer's Club for drinks. On one occasion, the CO, first sergeant, and company platoon leaders were going to the club, and I was invited. I told them I would not join them and mentioned on the tape, "maybe I should have, but I do not care." I wanted to make a tape while alone, and I said there was "not enough time to relax." Drinking at the club did not constitute relaxation to me.

On October 20, we went into the Michelin Rubber Plantation and set up ambushes for the night. No one came by. We went back to Dau Tieng for the day and repeated the process the next night. The Michelin rubber plantation was a large plantation of rubber trees. Rubber tree workers cut a groove around the trees like a barber pole to make the white rubber sap flow into buckets. They worked from 7:30 am to 4 pm, came by the truckloads, and were employed by the plantation owner. When we damaged any trees by gunfire or other means, the military had to reimburse the owner.

On October 22, the company set up a Rest Over Night position at about 4:30 pm. The CO asked if anyone had any reading material available. I sent up my Bible, but he replied that it was too heavy reading for him. However, my platoon sergeant, Sgt. Barnes, started reading the New Testament straight through. He said that he had never done that. The next day we were to use C-4 explosives and clear the area for a future LZ. We waited most of the morning for the C-4 to be brought out to us by chopper.

I subscribed to *Time* and *Newsweek* magazines while with the First Division. They gave me reading material during the boring times. An article in *Newsweek* described the 1960s as "the soaring sixties." That led me to tell Sylvia in a tape that I thought the 1970s would be "the searching seventies" when people would be searching for who and what they are. I also discussed that three great men of the century died in the 1960s. In order of greatness, my list was Churchill, MacArthur, and Eisenhower. I also noted that a fourth would have been Jack Kennedy. I said that I would consider making Eisenhower and Kennedy co-equals in third place; however, Ike would win out because he was a great military commander, president of a large university, a significant figure in the creation of NATO, and a US President. In the same tape, I suggested to Sylvia that when "she felt down about the whole thing" of us being separated, she should listen to the speech "Duty, Honor, Country" by General MacArthur to the graduating class of West Point in 1962. This discussion was evidence of my conservative interest in history and politics from my teen years. After, and because of, my year in Vietnam, my views changed dramatically in the pursuing years.

The barracks building, I lived in at the base camp had a TV, which sometimes worked. The picture was often snowy. One Sunday night, I watched *Bonanza* and *Mission*

Impossible. After it warmed up for 30 minutes, most of the snow disappeared. Instead of commercials between shows, there were military announcements. News was presented by military personnel wearing fatigues, broadcasting from Saigon.

In 1986 Sylvia and I visited a friend of ours from our church youth group in the 1960s. He was an Arizona highway patrol officer. One day, I went with him on the job in his patrol car. Sometime during the day, he commented that being a highway cop involved "long periods of boredom followed by short periods of adrenalin." That is how it was for us in Vietnam. Most of the time, we did not see any enemy soldiers. However, there were times when we did, and it was far from boring. The big problem was that things might be boring for several days, and then, in a few seconds, we were in a firefight. We never knew when one might happen.

My parents made a tape letter when they had Sylvia and the Ralph Bort family over for dinner in December. Ralph was Dad's best man at their wedding and a very good friend. All of them talked on the tape. Listening to that tape was almost like being at dinner. I wrote to Sylvia that I would not have taken $1,000 in place of having that tape.

10

Pine Ridge Fire Support Base

"I would like for you to pass a law so that there are no more swords or guns."

- Benjamin E. Hollar, age 6; letter to the President of the United States

On Sunday, October 26, we were airlifted to Fire Support Base Pine Ridge. It was about eight miles north of Dau Tieng, on top of a 900-foot-high mountain. It had belonged to the First Calvary Division, but they left it in shambles, and we were rebuilding it. At the center of Pine Ridge base was a tower about 25 feet high with the US flag flying on top. Near the tower was the TOC center, where planning and controls for the battalion was conducted. It was the brain and nerve center for battalion operations. Near the TOC were the battalion commanding officer's tent and bunker shelters for other officers.

One end of the base housed the 81 mm mortars, and the other was home to the 105 mm howitzer cannons. They supported the infantry units in the area. There were 12 bunkers around the base's perimeter, four armed with 50 caliber machine guns. There were also four M60 machine guns around the perimeter, and each GI had his M16 to secure the base. The M60 was a valuable weapon. In a firefight, it would put down a wall of steel. The bunker measured 12 feet long, nine feet wide, and five feet high. The command bunker had a telephone communication system connected to each of the 12 bunkers. My platoon sergeant and I stayed in that bunker. We had four wood bunks and one cot. We had a small light bulb powered by batteries that we "lifted" from a water trailer. Barbed wire circled the entire base, and there was radar at a location to watch out for movement around it.

Lt. Hollar with a M60

Each of the battalion's four companies spent time securing and working on it. The men did not like having to work there. They wanted a stand down and time to relax. That made my job all the more difficult since I was tasked with getting them to do the work. The company and battalion commanders would walk around the base to ensure everyone was working. So, I saw that, at least, the men looked busy working.

All in all, it was a break for everyone. The base was relatively secure, and we got two hot meals daily and a bunker to sleep. Our workday was from 7:30 am to 11:30 am and 1:30 to 5 pm. Benefits included two hot meals daily, cold sodas, and daily mail delivery.

One afternoon two jet fighters were putting in an airstrike that we could see from below the mountain. In formation, they buzzed the base and zoomed up. They put on an air show for us when they completed their strike.

After a few days, my platoon and the third were choppered out on an operation. The first remained to work and get the benefit of a roof over them and some hot meals. My men and I thought they got off easy and had the better deal. We would be sleeping with trees over our heads, C-rations for meals, and a higher possibility of getting killed. We were Casualties of War.

When we were in the field, we were resupplied every couple of days during the rainy season and less often during the dry season. The resupply chopper would also bring out a hot meal on those days. While working in the Michelin plantation, trucks would bring out the resupplies. Since it was near a village, the kids would come out to investigate. They would bring cokes out to sell, and another kid would come behind them selling ice. They had perfected capitalism.

Earlier he had been selling cokes to us

The chopper would also bring out mail. It was always in a red bag and greatly anticipated.

Red mail bag

Chow time in the jungle

Resupply chopper arriving
GI in the center is directing the pilot where to land

Hot meal with resupply

Meals on other days consisted of C-rations and anything that was sent from home. Some C-rations were much better than others, and it almost became a game to see who could get the best ones. An ideal breakfast for most guys was a can of peaches and a can of pound cake. It was tasty and coveted by almost everyone. I also liked them with coffee.

We could heat our meal using some C4, which was an explosive if detonated with a blasting cap but safe to burn by itself. It came in strips about six inches long, two inches wide, and an inch thick, wrapped in an olive-green cover. The burning process resulted in a hot yellow flame and gave us hot meals in minutes.

Since C4 was also an explosive, we used it to blast a landing zone for choppers. We would attach several sticks of the putty-like C4 around a tree and connect a wire with a blasting cap at the other end. The explosion would bring down a medium-size tree.

The 155 mm howitzers are noisy when they fire. They fire a lot, but I got used to it after a while. Otherwise, it is beautiful on the mountain. Looking to the south, I could see Dau Tieng and the rubber plantation. The Cambodian border was about 20 miles to the west.

On one operation, my platoon and November platoon went down the mountain. Lima platoon stayed up top as security. We were looking for any signs of an enemy coming up the mountain. We did not find anything.

During the summer of 1970, the *Stars and Stripes* newspaper reported that the base was attacked by 10 to 15 sappers planting explosives at critical locations. Four soldiers were killed, and another 12 were wounded. Damage was reported to be minor. Only a few months separated my platoon from being the victims of the sappers. It weighed heavily on my mind that those four soldiers could have been from my platoon or even that one of them could have been me.

One day one of my men told me that the Command Sergeant Major wanted to see me in the command center. I went to the center, saw the CSM, and asked him what he wanted. He said that an officer does NOT report to an NCO.

I felt so dumb. The men in the platoon got a good laugh out of it.

We often had spare time on our hands. That was particularly true on Pine Ridge but also correct other times. Sylvia sent me books to read during those times. While in Vietnam, I read *Hard Times, Literary Modernism, Christ in History, Born Free, The Jeweler's Eye, The Pearl, The Adventures of Tom Sawyer, Les Miserable, Brief Against Death, The Last of the Mohicans, Beyond All Passion, The Red Badge of Courage, Great Expectations, The Innocents Abroad, Moby Dick,* and *Of Mice and Men* among others.

During resupply, we got clean fatigues. Once when I was changing, I took everything out of my pockets. While I was not looking, one of the many kids stole my Bible. What a Vietnamese kid could do with an English translation of the Bible escapes me. Sylvia sent me another one. I kept the Bible in my top left pocket, thinking that it might slow down a bullet. I have heard of soldiers who had a Bible with a steel plate for a cover – to stop a shot.

I read a report of a US unit that went out to set up an ambush. After the shooting stopped, the men went out to see the results. One of the VC dead was identified as their barber back at the base camp. I expect this was more common than not.

When I went for a haircut at the base at Dau Tieng, I always carried a holstered .45 pistol. My thinking was that when the barber (a potential VC) got to the point of using the razor and made a threatening move, I might be able to roll to my left out of the chair so that I was facing him and put a couple of bullets through the heart of my would-be assassin.

11

A Day in the Jungle

How tragic it is to see old men who are unwilling to talk to potential adversaries but seem so ready to dispatch young people to fight and die."[14]

- General Wesley K. Clark, US Army

I received the cassette recorder from Sylvia on November 6 with a tape from her. She asked a lot of questions in this first tape. One was, "What is it like; what do you do all day there?" I took her question literally and told her in my first tape. It went something like this:

We woke up at daybreak, around 6:30 or 6:45. My breakfast was usually coffee and a can of fruit, and if I was lucky, I had enough pound cake from C-rations for each morning. We used C4 to heat the water for coffee. It was heated in an empty C-ration can of crackers. Before breakfast, the CO would make a "commo" check around 7 am. This means he would have his RTO call each platoon to make sure we communicated with each other on the radio. During the night, the CO's CP would make situation reports (sitreps) with each platoon to ensure someone at each post was awake.

---

[14] US Army General Wesley Clark (Ret.), "The Next War", *The Washington Post,* 16 September 2007, sec. B, p. 1.

Lt. Hollar

The CO would have told the platoon leaders the plans for the next day, either the night before or in the morning. I would relay that to my platoon sergeant and squad leaders. Everyone needed to know all the information that was available to us.

Around 8 am, the CO would order us to "saddle up" and then "move out." Saddle up meant to put our 50 or 60-pound packs on and get ready to go. Each day one of the three platoons would have the lead, meaning we would be the first in the column of three platoons to lead out. Lead was usually a more dangerous position since that platoon would most likely encounter the enemy first. Of course, that was not always the case, and enemy soldiers could appear to the left, right, or rear. The lead platoon generally had more responsibility and pressure by virtue of their location. Because of that, the CO rotated who had led between the platoons, each having led one day and rotating the next day.

Men of Mike platoon

Upon moving out in the morning, we would proceed with the orders for the day. It might be to do a bomb assessment operation. That would mean we would go to an area that had been hit by an Arc Light (B52 bombing raid) to see what was destroyed. It might mean we would do ground surveillance all day, where we moved through the jungle to see what we could see. It might mean that we went to an area where another unit had found a group of bunkers a month ago. We would be tasked with determining if anyone was there now or had been there recently.

We would take a break every 30 or 40 minutes for 15 minutes or so. The temperature and humidity were not conducive for extended walking. That was both a health and morale issue. A soldier with heat exhaustion would not be any help in a firefight. Sometimes, a break would be extended, such as when the CO would send out a squad on a cloverleaf assignment. That was when a squad of 10 or 12 men would leave the main unit and go out 100 or 150 meters to the main force's left or right to see any signs of enemy activity. They would call back over the radio to report their findings or lack thereof.

A possible scenario would be a call from the squad leader stating:

SL – Bravo 6, this is Mike 5, over.

CO – Mike 5, Bravo 6, what you got, over.

SL – Mike 5, we have three bunkers out 80 meters, maybe three to four months old, they have good overhead cover, firing ports face north, situated in a semicircle, main firing direction is 140 degrees. There is a major trail out from the ports about 20 meters—no recent activity at the bunkers or trail.

The CO would then decide whether the entire company would proceed to the site or continue elsewhere. Before that decision, he would have informed battalion HQ of the findings.

While the squad was doing its recon job, the rest of us would have a break in a place that might last 30 minutes or more. If it were with one of my squads, I would be keeping radio contact with them. When I had men "out there," it did not amount to much of a break for me. I kept thinking of what they might find or, worse, hit. Then the big question would be what to do. In moments like this I may have thought of the two army recruiters who helped put me there and made me a Casualty of War.

We would continue our operation until noon, when we would break for chow (lunch). Lunch would be 30 to 45 minutes. After lunch, we would continue with our assigned operation. The CO would start looking for a place to stop for the night around 4:00 or 4:30 in the afternoon. A location was usually found at about 5:30 or so each evening. The three platoons would split up and set up APs for the night. Likely spots would be on a trail, road, or an open area surrounded by jungle. The CO would tell me where he wanted me to set up and where the other platoons would be. This information needed to be passed on to everyone, so we did not kill each other in a firefight. Complete communication was a significant key to operating and surviving.

I would divide the platoon into four or five positions with five men. Each AP would have three men facing the road, trail, or open area, and two to the rear. If I thought the site looked unsafe, I would have four to the front. I would be with one of the APs, usually in the middle up front. I would distribute the two machine gunners to the far right and far left flanks so they could cover all of us.

In the November 6 tape, I told Sylvia, "It's not that bad, I guess. The worst thing is being wet at night from the rain. The first few weeks were dreadful because of all the rain in the rainy season." The rainy season in our area began in April and ended sometime in October. The thick jungle growth usually made it impossible to see the enemy. Often, we did not know who we were shooting. We only knew that whoever was out there was shooting at us.

I further told her, "I have not had to shoot someone point-blank myself. I know I would not hesitate to because... (pause)... you just do not do that if someone walks up to you." I went on to say, "Vietnam has some beautiful territory when seen from a chopper, but it is all scarred from artillery and bomb craters. I saw some beautiful large flowers recently while out in the field."

In early November, the Bravo Company was set up as a blocking force while Delta Company was searching out a bunker complex to our north. If any VC or NVA in the bunkers were trying to escape, we would nail them. We patrolled the same area five days earlier and found very fresh rice, medical supplies, and explosives. The bunkers appeared to be only two weeks old. This time it seemed that no one was there.

12

Kit Carson Scouts

"Organizations created to fight the last war better are not going to win the next."
- Lieutenant General James M. Gavin

In Vietnam, there was a Chieu Hoi program whereby VC could defect to the ARVN side, complete a training program, and then be assigned to ARVN or US units. They would be familiar with VC tactics and locations and could be valuable to an infantry unit. Some VCs chose to give up and utilize the program. During the war, some 200,000 enemy soldiers took advantage of the program. They were referred to as Kit Carson Scouts, and one named Duc was assigned to my platoon. He ate like a horse for being a typical, small, stature Vietnamese. On one occasion, when we were at the base camp, he had a roast beef dinner at the Chow Hall at 5:30. At 7:30, he was putting down a C-ration. One day a VC unit came to his village in Cambodia and told him to join them. They said that they would "crocodile" (kill) his parents if he did not. He did not want to join the VC, so he escaped and joined the KKK, a unit that sought only to maintain their security so they would fight anyone who threatened them, whether it was the VC, Americans, or South Vietnamese.

Duc, Mike platoon's Kit Carson Scout

When Duc first arrived, he did not know much English. As the weeks passed, he became easier to understand and helped us accomplish our mission. When the company went to the base camp at Dau Tieng for 24 or 36 hours, he would often not come back to join us for two or three days. One day I was kidding him about it and said, "GI gets one-day stand down, Duc gets three days, not fair." His reply led to me not bringing up the matter again. He answered with a bit of a tone, "GI come to Vietnam one year, Duc fight war 20 years!"

We had other Kit Carson Scouts assigned to us, but I remember Duc the best. He told me that the VC did not have radios like GIs. When a VC soldier was seriously wounded in the leg or arm, usually it would be amputated since they had no facilities to do otherwise. He said that many women in Cambodia served as medics, nurses, and doctors.

Duc used broken English to communicate with us. "Beaucoup" meant many, and "Ti Ti" meant little. "Number one" translated to very good, and "number ten 10" equated to very bad. "Same, same" meant precisely alike.

We were in the rubber plantation on November 14. We had set up for the night when we heard loud explosions near us. It turned out to be mortars that our Forward Observer (FO) (the person who directed mortar or artillery fire by radio for us) miscalculated and brought in on the 3rd platoon's position. Two men were killed and 11 others wounded. Some of the mortar rounds detonated in the rubber trees' limbs, sending shrapnel raining down onto the men. The FO was taken out of the field for his safety – no one would have thought much of him after that. By mistake, he had given his coordinates for the fire mission. I could hear the scream of "check fire, check fire" on the radio, which meant halt firing. A fateful evening highlighted the high cost of war and how, once again, we were Casualties of War.

Friendly fire events happen far too often in combat. Nineteen percent of the over 58,000 deaths during the war were not combat-related, highlighting the danger in a combat zone, including when no one was shooting at us.

One of the men killed was Staff Sgt. Howe, who was acting platoon leader. Their lieutenant platoon leader had been wounded a week earlier and was on his way back to the states since he had nerve damage, which would take months to heal. Nerves heal at the rate of one inch per month.

Tom McGrann was the leader of the first platoon at the time. In an April 25, 2012 email, he recalls:

> "I have some vague memories of the friendly fire incident. Instead of a fire fight, I remember the FO was with Lima and was registering fire for the night. At first, he gave the wrong coordinates but corrected himself after the first few rounds sounded too close. The next few rounds sounded about right to him, so he continued walking them in. The changes didn't get on the board, and the fatal rounds were based on the original coordinates, one klick off. Again, these are vague recollections; some may be hearsay or actual events on the ground.
>
> "One thing I do remember clear as day was November's position. As we entered, the young RTO seemed to be the only one not killed or wounded. He was in shock and described SSGT Howe's last moments. John was brand new to the company and fresh out of NCO training. He was standing up next to

a tree, and the RTO was seeking cover on the ground and telling him to get down. What happened next, I'm sure that haunts him until this day if he's still alive. Too gruesome to recall, but he insisted that we leave nothing and burn some stuff before we made a hasty departure."[15]

There was one 18-year-old soldier with my group who we called Dragoon that night. He was quite a goof-off and very immature. He tended to act up at the worst times. It hit me that one of the three killed was the platoon leader. After things calmed down from the friendly fire, I told the men where I kept critical items in case I were ever hit. I told them the location of my strobe light (for directing a helicopter to land at night) and other things I had. The young soldier looked at me and said, "Sir, if we ever need them, we will ask you for them." He could not have given me a better compliment.

We were choppered back to Dau Tieng on November 15 after being in the jungle for 13 days. We enjoyed a 36-hour rest.

While we were at the base camp in early January, my first sergeant told me that the battalion executive officer wanted to see me. When an officer from the battalion wants to see you, it is likely to be very bad or very good. I was not aware of anything I had done in the wrong category. So, I expected it would be an offer to take a staff assignment at the battalion.

It turned out that I was to be interviewed for a general aide position. I was to catch a flight to brigade headquarters at Lai Khe to be interviewed by a Major Byrd at S-1. That would have been an excellent assignment. However, Colonel Ansen, the battalion commander, and Major Kelly, the battalion S-1, did not want me to accept the position because the inflow of replacement lieutenants in the battalion had been halted, since it was likely that the First Division would be the next unit to be withdrawn in April. Also, the battalion was already short on lieutenants. He had to send someone to be interviewed, so it would be entirely up to me whether I

---

[15] Email from Tom McGrann, April 25, 2012.

accepted an offer. A total of nine lieutenants were interviewed for the position.

I interviewed with the brigade S-1 and told him: "I would like to have the job, but if it would put the battalion in a bind then I would just as soon stay in the battalion." My biggest desire was to get out of the field and away from being a platoon leader. The stress and danger were too great. However, I was loyal to the men in my platoon and battalion.

My mother responded to my decision: "You have been in the field enough; you need to get a staff job." From a distance of 10,000 miles, she sought to protect me.

Soon after this event, I missed out on another staff position in the battalion. A Lt. Jobs joined us and replaced Lt. McGrann as platoon leader of the Lima platoon. Four days after joining us, he got headaches and received a medical profile where he did not go out into the field. He was assigned to S-1 as an assistant. I was next in line for a staff job, so I missed another one. I had been in the field for four and a half months.

On a November 6 tape to Sylvia, I said that I had not yet seen any snakes but had seen a small tarantula. There was a wide variety of insects that we had to deal with. One particular problem was leeches. Unknown to us, they would crawl onto our skin and attach themselves. They were huge, reddish-black, slimy creatures we all hated and feared. They were challenging and painful to dislodge.

We saw many water buffalo from the air but only a couple while on the ground. Once we were on stand down at the base camp artillery, we had put out some rounds outside the perimeter during the night. In the morning, Lt. Col. Holt wanted a platoon to see what was there. My platoon got the assignment. We saw a young boy, maybe nine or 10, with his two buffalo. He was having a terrible time getting them to go where he wanted. I went to him and noticed he had a nasty cut on his hand that needed stitches. I had Doc, our medic (Ted Pettengill), look at him. Doc put antiseptic on it, and the boy was unhappy, thinking it would burn a lot. It must not have been too bad because he said, "no sweat, no sweat."

While out, we came upon a dead VC not far from the base perimeter. He had been shot in the cheek, and the bullet appeared to remain in his head. I noted that he had no blood seeping from the wound, and I thought that was strange. A few years ago, I read an article about head wounds. It said there would be no bleeding because the victim's heart had stopped instantly from the damage to the brain. It was not until then that I understood why the VC did not bleed. The strangest experiences and events bring it all back.

In the tape recording, I noted that we had been out in the jungle for 15 days on a mission, which was the longest time we had been out. It was too long to go without a shower, cold sodas, and hot meals. We were choppered back to Dau Tieng on Monday, November 3. The choppers were scheduled to come and pick us up at 12:30 pm. At 12:25, we got a radio message from the battalion that there was a "change of plans." That was nothing new for the army. The new arrival time was 3 pm. So, we were in an open field exposed to the hot sun and the enemy for an additional two and a half hours. At 3 pm, there was another delay. There was a B-52 strike going to our north, and the choppers needed to wait until they had an all-clear signal to fly to us. We felt the ground beneath us vibrate and shake from the strike. Finally, clearance was approved, and the choppers came at 5:15 pm.

We went back out to the jungle the next day at 2 pm. We were a blocking force for Delta Company pushing south towards us, checking for a VC base camp. If the VC tried to escape to the south, we would nail them. It turned out that the VC had left the base camp. This was a typical outcome of such an operation. It was as if they knew we would be coming. We were choppered back to the base camp on November 6, and the ships were on time, arriving a 4 pm.

One tape to Sylvia was made as I walked around the company area at about 9 pm. There were too many people in my barracks building for any privacy. I mentioned that pipes were sticking out of the ground with oil in them for burning at night. They did provide some light for getting around in the dark. While walking, I could see the base camp perimeter, consisting of multiple barbed wire rings.

When making a tape to Sylvia or my parents, I sometimes used military radio talk. In one to Sylvia, I used both sides of the tape. When I came close to the end of the first side, I said to her, "Break, Break, this is the end of the first side." That was the term we used on the radio when we wanted to quickly indicate to the receiver that I was changing the subject.

On one occasion, I told her my mind dwelt on things back home, mostly when I was at the base camp. There, I felt relatively safe, and my thoughts automatically turned towards her and home. I also said, "Out in the field, I think about things, but they are different things. I think about what I am doing, what might be ahead over the next hill, what we might be heading into, where my men are and what they are doing, and are they doing the right things."

In a combat zone being safe was relative. 58,220 Americans were killed during the war. Most were killed while out in the jungle fighting the enemy. Some, however, were killed at a base camp where they thought there was some safety. Mortars and rockets could be fired into the base, or they could be overrun by a large force. 10,786 (19%) of those killed were not from combat. They succumbed to accidents, illness, and other maladies.

In early November, I felt comfortable enough to take my Kodak Instamatic camera out on an operation. I began taking pictures in the beautiful jungle of South Vietnam. When we were extracted from the jungle, the choppers would often fly low over the Michelin Rubber Plantation. Such a flight displayed the beauty of the country.

Sunset in the jungle

Typical jungle growth

Lt. Ray Long joined the battalion in November. He and I were in the same training platoon in OCS. He was also a member of the OCS company Honor Council. I had come to know him very well, and we were friends. He was from Alabama and was assigned to Delta Company as a platoon leader. In early December 1969, I learned that Ray had been killed. He was the first person I knew well to be killed in Vietnam. The danger that engulfed me became clearer with Ray's death. Ray had planned to make the army a career. The US Army missed out on having an excellent officer and a gentleman joining their ranks.

On November 3, 1969, President Nixon gave a speech to the nation known as the "Silent Majority" speech, where he contrasted the antiwar groups with "the great silent majority." In a letter to Sylvia, I wrote:

"It was a well-prepared and delivered speech which expressed, I feel, the only rational view a responsible citizen could have. The telegrams and letters make it clear that the 'silent majority' has spoken."

In the same letter, I brought up the matter of having us having a child:

"Another important matter I think I'll bring up now is when exactly you think is the best time to plan our first child's birth? I've always heard that he should be born in the spring, so his (ok, her) early months are during warm months. What do you think? See, I'm getting down to dates now. I'm probably almost as anxious for one as you."

While the war had unceremoniously interrupted our lives, it could not stifle our planning for the future.

LT Guido was assigned to the rear job he had been waiting for. He would be in the S-5 Psychological Operations Office. On one occasion, when we had a 24-hour break at the base camp, Bill confided in me that the word around the battalion headquarters was that I was a good platoon leader. That was a great compliment. On November 9, a resupply chopper bought Guido's replacement to us, a LT McGrann.

On November 16, the company walked into the base camp from the Michelin, completing a 10-day mission. We had been looking for an NVA base camp. The S-2 office

(Intelligence) had said there was one where we had been, but we did not find one. S-2 intelligence was not always correct. After looking for a few days, we walked back into the Michelin and set up "bushes" each night. We saw a few VCs in the rubber and eliminated them.

13

Yesterday, Today, Tomorrow

"We shall draw from the heart of suffering itself the means of inspiration and survival."
- Winston Churchill

I wrote a letter to Sylvia's parents, Tom and Virginia Thornberry, saying, "In ways, every day here is just like yesterday was or tomorrow will be. We generally move around and operate in different areas. Then again, something different is always happening to give variety to the day. Sometimes the things that make for variety were such that it would be better if life were dull. I'm beginning to get some fascinating pictures. They will come close to showing what it is like over here except what it is like when there is shooting. I will never get that on film because there is too much to do at the time."

By November, my platoon was down to 25 men because of people going home or to other assignments, and we were not getting any replacements. On Thanksgiving Day, November 27, my platoon was still at Fire Support Base Pine Ridge. We had a big turkey dinner with all the trimmings. The rest of the company went into Dau Tieng for the holiday dinner. The battalion commander brought several female nurses from the Lai Khe base camp to the firebase. It was good to see some pretty faces up there for a change. In a tape home, I describe the menu as turkey, mashed potatoes, stuffing, gravy, sweet potatoes, peas, rolls, mixed nuts (I emphasized that it was mixed nuts, not just peanuts), cranberry sauce, assorted candy, tea, Kool-Aid, coffee, pumpkin pie, and minced meat pie. The US Army spared no expense to give us a Thanksgiving dinner with all the trimmings.

On Saturday, the platoon joined the rest of the company in Dau Tieng for the night. We left on Sunday for our 20-minute flight to Dian for our three-day in-country R&R. We were able to relax, catch up on letters, get hot meals, pool, movies, sleep in a bed with sheets, and just "hang out" for three days. Infantry companies got a R&R there about every 90 days. We returned to Dau Tieng on Tuesday, December 4, and returned to the jungle the same afternoon.

Lt. McCoy on left, and Sgt Knowles at Dian

Ted Pettengill (Doc) at Dian

By November, we were subjected to significant rain discomfort only once a week instead of daily as the rainy season had ended. Early in December, the temperature seemed to drop more at night. It must have been 60 degrees or less some nights. It was cool enough to have our sleeves rolled down, and some men would have their poncho liner wrapped around them early in the morning. By early October, the rainy season was beginning to end for the southern part of South Vietnam.

I sent Sylvia one of the maps I used when we were in the jungle or the Michelin plantation. I would refer to points on the map in my letters and tapes so she might feel a bit closer to me than the actual 10,000 miles. On a tape I made on December 11, I said, "Stop the tape now and get the map. Do you see Dau Tieng there at the bottom of the map? Take a look at the red road that goes off to the right. That road goes through the center of our area of operations (AO)."

On another tape, I told her: "The whole time we were out there in 10 days, we only saw three VC. My platoon got credit for one KIA (killed in action), and one Victor Charlie. It sounds insensitive to say, 'we got credit for one killed,' but the body count is what it was all about here."

While we were at Dau Tieng, the base camp had 20 to 25 incoming mortar rounds shot by the VC. We could hear the popping sound from their launch tubes as they fired each round. Based on the popping sounds, one of our artillery batteries determined their location and "blew them away."

Bravo Company was split into 12 squad-size ambush points in mid-December, which meant we were waiting for the enemy to come by. None showed up. If some VC came wandering by any of those ambushes, they would be in a real bind.

We often operated in the Michelin Rubber Plantation by setting up ambushes day and night. The mission was to stop the VC movement into and out of nearby villages, where they collected rice and other food to be taken back to their base locations. They could accomplish this because they often knew where we were and avoided us. The local villages supplied this information to them and aided them by giving them food. When we were resupplied near a village, the kids came out to us. The cute little Vietnamese girls running around went home and told Dad (probably a part-time VC) that they saw GIs at "such and such" place.

The month of December included two disappointments because I "almost got" a rear staff job. The Company Executive Officer (XO), Lt. McCoy, was relieved by the Company Commander at Lt. Col. Ansen's request. I was told at a Bravo Company reunion in 2006 that he had been doing drugs. Also, the First Sergeant and Supply Sergeant were relieved.

Lt. McCoy in front

This left an opening for a staff job in the company. The XO selection would typically be based on the lieutenant who had the most time in the field, which would have been me. However, I was not selected. The first platoon leader, Tom McGrann, was a first lieutenant but had three weeks less in the field than I. His MOS was Adjutant General (AG), and he was detailed to the infantry for two years. His selection was a big letdown. I recall my men saying, "Now, Lieutenant, you know what it is like when you don't get a rear job." I sure did.

Bravo Company returned to the base camp by choppers on December 22 after a nine-day operation. We had less than 24 hours at the camp since we were going back out to the Michelin the next day.

On an operation before Christmas, we were out for nine days before returning to base camp. On a tape to Sylvia, I gave her a summary of where we were:

"We were in the open area identified by grid 52/54. We were near AP 6 on the map's red road due north. We were to stay around the villages in the area to stop the VC. We moved north into the rubber plantation and saw no VC while out. A few days before that, the entire battalion was on an operation just south of the mountain range."

The company killed its first VC in about a month on Christmas Eve. True, there was an Allied and NVA cease-fire; however, theoretically, it was a defensive move. The third platoon had set up two Claymore mines near one of their ambushes. A lone VC tripped the wire, and the explosion killed him.

My platoon came upon a road on New Year's Eve, and my point man spotted a VC. He signaled to the rest of the platoon, and everyone dropped to the ground; and we opened fire when they came closer to us. There were four VCs. We wounded one, and the others escaped. We could see that the prisoner was in a lot of pain. When Captain Boyden arrived at our location, he said, "Did you give him morphine?" We had, and a chopper was called to take him to the base camp as a prisoner of war.

In a February 4, 1970 letter to my pastor and church members, I presented them with an opportunity: "If you're tired of getting up at 6 am for school or work, join the infantry and come over here. Normally, I don't get up until 7 am or even later. There is no rush hour traffic to get to work; however, the ground serves as your mattress, so there are definite disadvantages."

Bravo Company headquarters at Dau Tieng

In November, the news media became aware of the events at My Lai in March 1968. It was when Lt. Calley and his men murdered over 500 Vietnamese. The army did all it could to cover it up, but it became public. I only knew the basic information about it. In a December 11 tape to Sylvia, I stated that such a thing "...could happen to any one of us. The stress of heavy combat is something the average person would not comprehend, analyze, or judge unless they have been in it." I ended my thoughts to her with, "Let he who is without guilt cast the first stone."

We only knew what we were being told; that was not the whole story. In one of my letters to my pastor and church members, I wrote:

"I am more than aware of the possibility of this happening. Perfectly normal young American soldiers can do what they were accused of doing. The line between friend and foe, enemy or ally, is very thin in this war. I am afraid that under the most pressing of circumstances, as must have existed at Song My, that line could have been erased."

Just before I came home, I told Sylvia in a letter that "I did not do anything I was ashamed of while being in Vietnam." My conscience was clear. There are some things, however, that I did that disappoint me now. They were mistakes that I made. Unfortunately, mistakes are always Casualties of War.

14

Christmas in South Vietnam

"We have good corporals and sergeants and some good lieutenants and captains, and those are more important than generals."

- William Sherman

There was a Christmas ceasefire from December 24 at 6 pm until Christmas Day at 6 pm. As usual, each platoon set out booby traps for the night near where they were located. Ironically, the booby trap did not recognize the ceasefire and detonated when several VCs wandered by. Theoretically, no one was shot. The death was from a booby trap bomb.

We were out in the field on Christmas Day. We could either stay in the field or walk into the base camp for Christmas dinner. We voted on the issue and decided to stay out since a round trip walk would be four hours of tromping in the heat. We had an excellent traditional Christmas dinner. The colonel came out with a couple of chaplains. We had an artificial tree brought out, which we decorated. Also, our forward observer carried a folding Christmas tree. The Red Cross sent out little cloth bags containing writing paper, pens, candy, gum, soap, peanuts, recording tape, and books.

In a December 25 letter to Sylvia, I wrote: "So the protestors hate war. They don't know the half of it. No one could hate war more than the soldiers who fight - not even the mothers, fathers, and wives. Wars will not cease in this

Age, but good men's idealism and hope may help reduce their terror. Plato is still correct when he wrote, 'Only the dead have seen the end of war.'

"On the day that we celebrate the birth of the Prince of Peace, we can see the light at the end of the tunnel, the final toll gate as we speed down the highway. I see smiling faces and gleaming eyes of those going home early and hopes of those in the classrooms who may not have to come. Maybe, we see the beginning of the end. What more could one require of Christmas 1969?"

On many resupply operations, a chaplain would come out on the chopper and conduct a short service. I would go to all of them, like some of my platoon's men. Most of the guys who came to the services were from my platoon, and I wondered if they came because they wanted to or because I did, and they thought they should. In this case, I guess the reason does not matter.

There were both Protestant and Catholic chaplains. They would provide a hymn book for singing, and have prayer and a 15 to 20-minute sermon.

The messages presented by the chaplains were about our attitudes. They did not usually address the matter of salvation, which one would have thought would be a prime subject in a combat environment.

Chaplain visits during resupply

Captain Boyden started a company meeting at 6:30 pm with the platoon leaders and sergeants on one stay at the base camp. On one tape, I noted that it lasted until 10 pm and could have been at least an hour shorter. About halfway through the meeting, someone mentioned needing a beer. Sgt. Jim Fletcher, my platoon sergeant, went to get them. As he was about to leave, I said, "don't forget one coke." He replied, "Oh yes, six beers and one coke."

Jim was from Michigan and had graduated from "shake and bake" school. That term described the training GIs received at that Army school. I believe it was a school of several weeks in length where the graduates came out as E-5's and ready to be squad leaders. I guess, in one sense, I was a "shake and bake" lieutenant, although my training was 23 weeks. On another occasion, Jim told me that his wife should have married me since she does not drink.

On the 14th, the battalion got a new CO – Colonel Ansen. Colonel Holt went to a position at the brigade level. Sometimes when we were at the base camp in Dau Tieng, Colonel Holt would host a dinner for all the officers. They were called Drac Mess Nights, and I went to several. We sat at a long table with the colonel at the head. Before the dinner began, there would be a toast with wine. I took the opportunity to taste it but found it not very pleasant.

There was a dinner held to wish him well in his new assignment. He noted the battle on October 2 that Bravo Company had endured and that Alpha Company had swept through the next day to evaluate the situation. He said that the day before he and his pilot had flown over our operations area, he pointed out place after place where the battalion had come through when the chips were down.

The dinners were enjoyable unless we had just come in that day for one night. Then I would rather be on my own.

Bob Hope came to Vietnam during Christmas in 1969. He performed at Lai Khe, the division headquarters, on December 22. My platoon was able to go. His opening line was, "Well, here we are in Lai Khe again – those hijackers are never around when you need them." A lot of the guys made signs welcoming the show. One read, "Welcome Bing Crosby." He referred to the men at the show as "last year's winners in the draft lottery." He entertained us with a barrage of his "one-liners." Of course, he had beautiful women there, including dancer Suzanne Charny, singer Theresa Graves, the 13 beautiful "Golddiggers," and singer-actress Connie Stevens. I remember to this day her moving rendition of the song "Bill."

Suzanne Charny at the Bob Hope Show

Connie Stevens with some of the troops at the Bob Hope Show

Neil Armstrong at the show

Astronaut Neil Armstrong was also with the group, but most eyes were on the girls. Hope had 83 members in his troupe that year. He ended all of his programs with everyone singing "Silent Night." Captain Boyden commented that there was probably not a dry eye in the group when it was sung. I suspect he was correct. The show was rebroadcast in the states on January 15.

Joe Fair was a member of Company A in the battalion. At a battalion reunion, he told me that his company was part of the security for the Bob Hope show. A big heap of thanks to Joe and Company A!

While we were in the field the week after Christmas, battalion headquarters called the CO and said we had a "change of mission." The CO told me to bring my platoon to his location right away. Everyone assumed the worse when word spread through the platoon about the change. To a GI, a mission change was never good and would likely be quite harmful. When we got to the CO, he told me he did not have more information about the mission. Our orders were to walk back to the base camp at Dau Tieng and wait on the airstrip where the choppers took off for air assaults. That news confirmed our worse fears; we would be air assaulted into a nest of a hundred VC instead of getting a 24-hour stand down. In a tape to my parents, I said, "We were furious now, and the whole company felt like throwing the country of Vietnam right into the ocean."

When we did receive orders, our anger increased. We were to be the "ready reaction force" for a visit by Vice President Agnew to Fire Base Keen. If the base were attacked or mortared while he was there, we would be air assaulted to it to pursue the attackers. We arrived at the airstrip at 2 pm and waited on the hot tarmac until 5:30 before getting the "all clear" that the VP had left the base. Trucks came out to the airstrip and took us to our company area. We had a 24-hour break before being airlifted back into the jungle on January 3.

Near the end of December, I learned that my dad had an accident at work. He was a carpenter foreman at the Naval Research Laboratory near Washington DC. He was using a new drill press that had a defective drill bit. The bit was some 12 or more inches long. It bent halfway when he started the motor, making a nasty slice across his forearm. He was out of work on sick leave for several months. I hated not being able to be home for him and Mom.

Around 3 pm, my platoon came upon a road on New Year's Eve, and my point man spotted a VC. We all dropped to the ground and began firing when he was close. It turned out to be four, and three got away. One was wounded. The Allied ceasefire did not start until 6 pm, but if it had been 6:15, it would have been the same story. All this to say that a ceasefire, a truce, to the ground soldier, is an absolute farce with his life on the line.

15

Hawaii Bound

"When a general makes no mistakes in war, it is because he has not been at it long."

- Tureene

In mid-December, I received my R&R assignment for going to Hawaii in January. I would meet Sylvia there. Usually, one or two allocations came to the company for out-of-country R&R each month. In December, the company received four. I almost did not get one until one of the men planning to go in January changed his mind. Our dates for Hawaii were January 7 to 13, 1970. As a result of the timing, I did not return to the company's field since I was to report to Dau Tieng on the 4th. I flew from there to the Dian R&R center and on the 6th to Camp Alpha. I left for Hawaii on the 7th at 10 am and arrived in Hawaii at 5:30 am.

Sylvia and I discussed and looked forward to our rendezvous in Hawaii in tapes and letters from September through December. It was a constant subject on both our minds. One of the tapes I said it would be "Halloween, Thanksgiving, Christmas, and New Year's all rolled into one."

One of the housekeepers in the company area was a Vietnamese girl named Susie. When I told her I would meet my wife in Hawaii, she was about as happy about it as I was. I showed her some pictures of Sylvia; she went "crazy" with joy and thought it was terrific.

We planned for Sylvia to arrive in Hawaii on the 6th, and I would come on the morning of the 7th. In a tape to Sylvia, I told her to bring about $700 in traveler's checks. The Army paid for my flight, and Sylvia received a 50% discount for an Army R&R trip.

We stayed at the Colony Surf Pavilion, which was on the ocean in Honolulu. It had three restaurants in the facility. We had a corner room with an ocean view, a Diamond Head view, and a balcony. The room cost $20 a night, which was about 50% off for service personnel and was lovely. I had told Sylvia that I wanted to rent an air-conditioned Ford Mustang. Instead, all they had for us was a run-of-the-mill sedan with a dent on the side.

The night before I was to leave for Vietnam, we went to dinner at a rotating restaurant. We had a great time that night. The waiter was a little "snooty." Since we were leaving the following day, Sylvia was not very hungry. The waiter came and saw that she had quite a bit left on her plate. He asked if she wanted a brochette. Neither of us had any idea what that was. Sylvia thought that if she could not eat what she had, she certainly did not want anymore – brochette or otherwise. She thanked him and said no. The waiter looked taken back and said, "Madam, your dinner will be on the house." By brochette, he meant a doggy bag. Well, we got a free dinner out of the experience.

My flight back to Vietnam left from Gate 18 of the Hawaii International Airport. Sylvia had left 90 minutes earlier. Before, I saw that about half of the passengers waiting were GIs with their wives. Most of them were crying. On a tape to Sylvia, I said, "I found it sad."

On my night flight to Hawaii, there were always 20 to 30 overhead lights on at any time, and everyone was excited about the trip. My flight back was also at night and very different. There was little talking, and there were no overhead lights on during the night. We had one stop in Guam for refueling. I used the occasion to purchase three small notebooks from the PX to use on operations. I slept for seven hours on the trip.

We arrived at Tan Son Nute airbase at 8 am on January 15, and I caught an Army bus to Di An two hours later. From there, it was a short flight on a Caribou aircraft to Dau Tieng. Upon arriving at the base camp, I walked to the Bravo Company area.

When I got there, the company was loaded on trucks to take to the airstrip for a chopper flight to Pine Ridge. If I had rushed, I could have joined them but chose not to. I caught a flight to the firebase the next day. While there, I told Captain Wells that I had just returned from R&R. He replied, "I could tell - it will take about a week to get back in the groove."

I was assigned to a bunker with other lieutenants. It had four wood bunks and a cot and was about 12 feet long and nine feet wide with a five-foot ceiling that was two feet thick. We had telephone lines to each of the other bunkers and a switchboard in the command bunker. We stole tiny light bulbs from the water trailer, hooked them up to batteries, and had some light at night. We worked six or seven hours daily, and the men had the rest of the time to themselves.

When I returned to the company, I learned that Corporal Michael Dalton and Specialist Gerald Dasen of the 3rd platoon went out from their overnight mechanical ambush location one morning to recover their Claymore mines on the road. They set them up as booby traps in case any NVA came by. They became disoriented and forgot where the mines were located. They tripped the wire, and the explosion killed both of them. Bob Brown remembers the incident this way:

> "It was early morning, and my platoon (Mike Platoon) was to take the point for the day. The company had set up platoon-size ambushes in the Michelin Rubber Plantation the night before. As we were about to leave our "bush" site and headed to pick up Lima Platoon, we heard an explosion that sounded like Claymores in Lima's direction. The platoon RTO Beavers told us that their Claymore ambush wounded two of Lima's men. When we arrived, "Doc" joined Lima's medic in tending to the wounded. They were lying on the road. They were walking on the road to retrieve their ambush. I think one died before the

dust-off arrived and the other on the way to the hospital."[16]

I remember thinking, "I should have been there." However, they were not in my platoon, so there was nothing that I would have done or could have done to prevent it. Still, I felt like it would have made a difference. Even going on, R&R had its demons.

It had to do with platoons deploying mechanical ambush devices such as the one that killed two of our men. As a result, the battalion issued a report on January 14, 1970, titled "Lessons Learned: Mechanical Ambushes." The report read:

> "This unit has employed mechanical ambushes (Mech APs) for 30 days. Each company was extremely hesitant during the first 15 days and installed only four to six per night. During the last 15 days, 12 to 13 per company have been employed nightly. A minimum of two Mech APs is set out with each manned AP. The battalion will usually have between 50 and 60 Mech APs in operation on an average night. One company (Co. C) has at various times set out 30."

During those 30 days, 16 Mechs were detonated, nine were detected by the enemy and avoided, animals detonated five, and two fired for unknown reasons. The Mechs killed nine enemy soldiers during the 30 days. US casualties resulting from the Mechs were five wounded and three killed. The enemy tampered with one of the devices. The report stated, "The mechanical AP is a very efficient but potentially dangerous means of interdicting enemy movement." All three platoons in Company B frequently set out Mech APs at night.

In a January 17 letter to Sylvia, I wrote, "Several of the guys have said they're glad to see me back and feel a lot better. They seem to have had quite a time of it while I was gone." On this day, we got a new guy in the platoon. He had a Master's degree in chemistry. I thought it was a waste of knowledge and talent. Then again, the army was wasting my degree in accounting except that we had to count the number of bodies we killed.

---

[16] Email from Bob Brown, January 3, 2009.

While in Vietnam, Sylvia worked as a salesperson in the women's department at Woodward and Lothrop, a department store. In a letter, she complained about having to take inventory. She told me that it was "dumb." Since I majored in accounting, and one of my courses was auditing, I knew the need to take inventory. I told her that "dumb" accountants like me required it.

In January, I subscribed to *Newsweek* and *Time* magazines. I wanted to keep up with the news "back in the world."

On January 25, 1970, I received a promotion to first lieutenant. The requirements to become a first lieutenant in Vietnam were one, you have been a second lieutenant for one year, and two, you are still breathing. Yes, you have to be in good standing, but not much more. My pay increased from $429 to $535 a month, and the housing allowance went from $110 to $120. I wrote Sylvia, "If I re-enlisted in January 1971, my annual pay would be $9,000 a year."

Upon being promoted, taking everyone to the Officer's Club was customary, and buying everyone a round of drinks. The CO had told Lt. McGrann that he would lose his commission if he did not get me drunk. When I heard that, I jokingly told Tom, "You know you are going to lose your commission tonight." He replied, "Yes, I know."

Lt. McGrann in the background

Bravo Company crossing an old bridge

My platoon Sergeant, Bob Barnes, was not what you would call a "religious" man. Nor would I describe him as the opposite. In January, he told me he planned to read the New Testament. He had never done that but was going to try. I do not know whether he accomplished that goal.

On January 20, I wrote Sylvia telling her that I had completed reading *Hard Times* and told her that I had "found the deeper meaning and implications of novels to be very interesting ever since taking a literature course in college. That was especially true as they affected social injustice. I added, "Maybe I should write a book about being in Vietnam. I could call it "Hard Times," which also involves injustices.

Sometimes in a tape letter to Sylvia, I would walk her through a mapping exercise. One discussion went like this:

"Are you ready for your map lesson on what we did during our recent operation? So, get your map out." I would stop recording to give her a chance to find the map I sent her.

"OK, I bet you did not get it! So, I'll give you another chance, so go get it now. OK, I bet you still did not get it, so you can come back later to use the map."

"Anyway, we started at grid coordinate 574698 at a small LZ." Then I went on to describe what we did.

16

Rear Assignment

"To introduce into the philosophy of war a principle of moderation would be an absurdity. War is an act of violence pushed to its utmost."

- Clausewitz

Rumors had begun in December that the First Division would be one of the first to be withdrawn. Officers were allowed to make three preferences for our next assignment. I requested the following locations:

- Saigon Support Command (Administrative position)
- MACV (Advisor job or administrative)
- 25th Infantry Division (Like the First Division. This would be my best choice of the units here, so I included it to keep from getting one that would be particularly bad.)

I knew a unit was located at or near Long Binh, which was only 20 miles south of Saigon, so I figured it would be safer than someplace up north near the DMZ. I thought the unit was the 198th or 196th Light Infantry Brigade, but I was unsure. Since I was skeptical, I did not put either on my preference list.

In a January 28 tape, I told Sylvia that we came into the base camp on the 27th after 15 days. I told her to "get your map out" and gave her an account of the operation. We were airlifted to Grid 574698, and my problems began. I learned that one of our M-60 machine guns needed the bolt replaced. It was supposed to be wired in but was not. It was something I should have known about but did not. A chopper brought out a new barrel for the weapon. I considered it unacceptable to proceed on an operation with only one M-60.

During this operation, each of the three platoons operated on our own in different locations. On the 27th, we met at an LZ for pick up to come back to Dau Tieng. I expected we were close to the rendezvous point, but I did not know the exact location. I held the platoon up and sent a squad of five men out to find the precise opening where the choppers would be coming in. Through experience, I learned that I was very good at map reading. I remember doing well in it during OCS training.

I called the CO so he would know what I was doing and where we were. He passed that information to the Battalion headquarters. Captain Boyden called me back and said the battalion was saying I was in the wrong place and had moved farther away from the LZ instead of closer since my last radio report. I rechecked my map and the surroundings and was convinced that I was where I thought I was. The CO, battalion, and I went back and forth about my location for 20 minutes. Over the preceding four months, I trusted myself with my map reading. I found that I was usually very accurate in that area.

Capt. Boyden in center on the radio. John Cirjak behind him on the radio.

So, now I had a squad out in the jungle, and I did not know where they were. They did not know where they were, we had no radio contact, and now battalion headquarters was telling me I did not know where I was. By this time, my anger had morphed into fear and fury.

While I was trying to deal with multiple problems, my friends back home were thinking about their date on the weekend; what nightgown their wives or girlfriends would wear that night; how the contract negotiations were going at the office; why the bus was 12 minutes late that morning; why John got the last promotion instead of him; when their parents would come visit; and why the hell we were in Vietnam.

Finally, the battalion called and said I was right, so half of my problem was solved. After about 45 minutes, the missing squad got the radio back online and found their way back to the platoon. I was not happy with them for giving us such a scare.

In a January 31 letter, I described to Sylvia two days of a fouled-up operation:

"You wouldn't believe how messed up this operation has been. On Thursday, we landed at grid coordinate 587583, walked to 590600, and spent the night. The Brigade Commander had some "007" idea of having a plane fake a crash into that open area and have us blow up some Claymore mines to make it look natural. Then we were to circle the open space and set up around it to get Charlie as he came to investigate. ZOOW! Grab your map, and I will give you a run down.

"Anyway, the mission was canceled, and we walked from the open area 590580 to 560590 and then to 550570. Today we came down to 546545 in the Michelin. Therefore, we are back in the rubber again. It was very rough walking the last two days. We had to have a chopper bring us 30 gallons of water today.

"The policy has changed to resupply every three days, so we are due one the next day. I need some new pants – I had this problem: they split in the rear two days ago. Also, it rained miserably last night!"

17

Cease Fire

"Lord, Lord, how this world is given to lying!"
- Henry IV, Part 1, Act 5

By February, our AO had been so well pacified that each of the three platoons in the company would be air assaulted to different locations. Each would check out their areas and report our findings to the company commander. We would not reconnect with the company until choppers picked us up and deposited us onto the base camp where the rest of the company would go.

On February 15, we were located near Saigon. Choppers flew us to a position where we were attached for a week to the 2nd of the 2nd, a mechanized battalion. Their base camp was also at Dau Tieng. We rode the Armored Personnel Carriers (APC) for a while, then got off and set up for the night nearby.

After dark, but before we went to sleep, the APCs started firing their 50-caliber machine guns directly over our heads. We could tell by the tracers that they were shooting about 15 feet above us. Everyone immediately dropped flat on the ground. I said to my RTO, "Give me that damn horn." I radioed the CO and told him they were firing right over our heads. The calls went out to "Cease Fire." Fortunately, they stopped before anyone was hit. I am unsure what the mix-up was, but it scared us all out of our wits. I knew from training that if one of us were struck in the shoulder by one or two 50-caliber bullets, it would separate his arm from the torso. It would have been horrid. The bullet in the shell casing is 5.45 inches long and .8 inches in diameter.

Lt. Hollar

We learned that the First Infantry Division was the next unit to withdraw from Vietnam at the end of March in late January. Our division commander said we "had worked ourselves out of a job." That would not mean I would get to go home since I would still have five months left. I would go to another unit.

The company was scheduled to have a stand-down at Dau Tieng beginning February 8, but it was canceled at the last minute because Charlie Company had to be air assaulted into an LZ, and Lt. General Miloy, the division commander, said it was canceled due to excess division air time and fuel consumption. In a tape to Sylvia, I referred to that excuse as "a bunch of nonsense." Instead of entering the base camp, we set up our usual ambushes on the night of the 8th. We received orders at 9 am the following day, and we would be picked up by choppers and airlifted back to the battalion HQ. That morning the time was changed to 11 am, and as I said on a tape, "miracles of miracles at 11 am, the first four ships came in." At 2 pm that afternoon, an awards ceremony was held for Bravo Company by the battalion commander, and a number of the men received awards.

On February 20, a Chinook helicopter brought 30 new men to the company. They were from the 2nd to the 28th. Nine were assigned to me. That was the first unit to process out, so they recycled the men with too much time left to go home back into the division. They brought my platoon strength back up to 35. They were to stay with us until we went to Dian on March 17 to begin out-processing.

I considered the withdrawal a good thing except for the 50,000 who would be the last ones to leave if Hanoi were to launch an offensive. I had no desire to be among the last to leave.

During the week of March 11, my platoon found eight brand new bunkers measuring five feet by 15 feet. Each was five or six feet deep. Along with the bunkers was a tunnel where radio batteries and rice were stored. It was clear that the enemy was still around. The administration and the American public may have been closing their eyes, but the reality of the situation was that "Charlie" was there to stay.

My battalion led the entire division for the first quarter of 1970 in the number of enemies killed with the least casualties. That was a prime indicator of the quality of the unit. It is the ultimate score sheet of an infantry unit's effectiveness. During that period, my company worked directly with two other battalions in the division, and without question, the 1/2nd was far superior in professional capability. I was thankful to be with an outstanding unit, even considering what we were required to do was sickening. I had become a Casualty of War.

Lt. Waller became our new Company CO. He was a young Afro-American who graduated from OCS and had four children at home. He took over the company very smoothly.

Lai Khe became our new battalion base camp. It was also located in a rubber plantation, so there was plenty of shade for the rare occasions when we would be there. We traveled by truck to the new camp from Thunder II fire support base. The truck convoy was a miserable, rough, and dusty ride.

Around this time, I wrote in a letter to Sylvia: "I'm getting kind of tired of stomping around in the jungle. If my next unit does not place me in a staff job, I will let them know of my dissatisfaction quickly."

We were out in the jungle in early March, with each platoon setting up in separate locations. I told my platoon sergeant to have each of the three squads set up separately. He asked, "Why don't we set up all together tonight?" We were all aware that the First Division would withdraw in a few weeks, so no one wanted to be subject to many risks. The S-3 was above us in his chopper, giving me instructions. So, I told the platoon sergeant that I would run it by the S-3. I knew it would be rejected, but it gave me another opportunity to let the men know that I listened to them and was open to their ideas. The S-3 replied: "Now, lieutenant, let's keep things professional and set up separately." I did not score any points with him, but I did not care. I was not interested in being promoted to captain since I was not staying in the Army.

18

Man on a Trail

"It is impossible to kill without emotional investment. The enemy must in some way be dehumanized, degraded to less than full human status."
- William Mahedy [17]

Ordinary people do not desire to kill other people. In war, the soldier is expected, even ordered, to do just that. In the army's Basic and Advanced Infantry Training, the recruit was taught the techniques of killing another man. It may be by bullets, grenades, machetes, bayonets, or hand-to-hand combat with one's bare hands. We were forced to scream, "Kill," "Kill," "Kill," when performing various training functions, particularly when marching. It can be a personal survival issue to kill others during a war.

The December issue of *Newsweek* included an article concerning the GI and the "dink" complex. It becomes necessary for the soldier to view his enemy as something other than entirely human. The Germans were "Krauts," and the Japanese were "Japs" in World War II. In the Vietnam War, the enemy was called "Gooks" or "Dinks." Other derogatory terms also used are "Nips," "zipperheads," "slopes," and Huns." It was easier to kill a Gook or Dink than a 20-year-old Vietnamese young man with a mother, father,

---

[17] William Mahedy, *Out of the Night – The Spiritual Journey of Vietnam Vets*, (Ballentine Books) 17.

brothers or sisters, and probably a wife or girlfriend. After contact, the question from our higher levels was, **"How many Gooks did you kill today?"**

I never got used to using those terms. I did all I could not to use them. I tried to refer to the enemy as the Viet Cong (VC) or North Vietnamese Army (NVA) soldiers. I do not know if anyone ever noticed that. I do not recall anyone mentioning it. Most, if not all, of the men in my platoon used the other names frequently.

The Viet Cong and NVA soldiers were destined to kill American soldiers as much as we were to kill them. When a unit has some of its men killed, it can negatively affect the soldiers' psyches. Sometimes the effects of your buddy dying from a Viet Cong booby trap are too much to bear. The element of vengeance can come into play. Sometimes it got the best of the noblest of soldiers.

On October 31, 1969, the company came upon a freshly used trail at about 4:30 in the afternoon. Captain Saunders, our company commander, ordered my platoon (2nd) and the 1st to set up an ambush for the night. The third platoon was pulling security on Pine Ridge. I had just finished checking the position of my machine gunner. I wanted to be sure he was in a good spot if we needed him that night. Then I walked out to the trail to get a last look to remember where everything was placed. I came back to the position of the ambush and turned around. As I turned, I saw an NVA soldier on the trail about 20 feet from me through the jungle growth. I saw that he had a Rocket Propelled Grenade (RPG) launcher (like what was used by the insurgents in the Middle East) – but it was not armed with the warhead and ready to fire. Terrified, I dropped to the ground and brought my M-16 up to fire. **IT JAMMED**! I tried Immediate Action (what the army taught us to do when a weapon jams). Of course, that did not work. Immediately to my right was Lloyd Woods (an African American soldier in my platoon) with his machine gun. For the first time in my life, I wanted someone dead. Lloyd let out several bursts – and – the NVA soldier was no longer an issue. What if the NVA had his RPG armed and ready to fire…. If Woods had not been there…

Lloyd Woods on a happier day

Captain Saunders was wounded in the leg during the same exchange of fire. Lt. Guido, the senior platoon leader, became the new company commander. A medivac chopper took Capt. Saunders for medical help. He did not return to the company.

When the shooting stopped, one of my men asked me why I did not fire. I told him that my rifle had jammed. One of the guys near me was Ron Farrow. He and I were at the 2008 Bravo Co. reunion. He told me that when my rifle jammed, "your face turned white as a sheet."

In an email to me, Paul James described the condition of the dead enemy soldier, writing that his head had been "blown apart." I do not remember that. I expect it is hidden somewhere deep inside my 85 billion neurons. When I recorded the event on my tape diary, I said I needed "to profit from the experience and move on" and "Tomorrow is Another Day."

We moved back a distance, and Lt. Guido had the company set up in a large circle during the night. It was a long night. I had plenty of time to contemplate that the NVA soldier "I effectively killed" had a mother and father. He probably had brothers and sisters, a girlfriend or wife, and possibly children.

Captain Saunders was replaced by Captain Boyden, the company commander of the Headquarters Company. Several of us were concerned that he was more of an administrative person and not cut out to be a combat commander. We talked among ourselves, saying: "He is going to get us all wiped out; get us killed." Some of the ways he did things were strange. Fortunately, he seemed to catch on to what to do after a while, and things looked better.

19

Relative Safety

"Those who cannot remember the past are condemned to repeat it."

- George Santayana

At the end of February, I learned I would be going to the 199th Light Infantry Brigade Brig. Gen. William Ross Bond commanded the 3,000-man brigade. The base was 25 miles northeast of Saigon and only a few miles from Bien Hoa Air Base, where I had landed seven months earlier. On a tape to Sylvia, I declared, "For the first time, the Army gave me a break." I described the assignment to Sylvia in a tape as "quite excellent.

It was not long before I realized that my assignment would be vastly improved over the previous six months. Captain Jiran was the Personnel Management Officer, and he made all the personnel assignments. I described it to Sylvia in a March 25 letter:

"I don't believe I could have handpicked a better job assignment than the one I got." The section consisted of a major, two captains, myself, and several enlisted men. My accounting major was the deciding factor since S-1 handled the brigade's monetary funds. Finally, the Army was using what I was trained to do. One of the captains had friends with Arthur Andersen & Co. in New York. I was also a general project officer for the Brigade Commanding General, i.e., having plaques, trophies, and awards made. It entailed going to Saigon now and then. I was responsible for auditing the brigade's 25 or so monetary funds each month. Audits of the funds were to be completed by the 10th of the month, so I was swamped for the first 10 days of the month. This meant that I did not have much to do for some weeks. So, I would take some time off then.

A significant part of my job was to have plaques made for special occasions such as for promotions of officers and other events. I would go to a shop in Saigon to order them. Two days after beginning the job, I had gone to Saigon twice to purchase materials and order plaques. When I went to Saigon, one of the men in our office drove the jeep. On one trip, we walked by a massage parlor. He asked us to wait for him while he was in there. There was a massage parlor at the base camp at Dau Tieng also. Some of my men visited the place. When someone wanted sex, they would call it "Boom, Boom." I never entered their doors.

I had a room (with mattress and sheets), and for $10 a month, I had my laundry done, room cleaned, bed made, and boots polished by a Vietnamese hooch girl. At first, I had difficulty getting one of the girls to work for me. She said she "had too many men to work for." She was cleaning for eight at the time and thought that was too many. After talking for a while, she said, "you go to the boss," who was Lt. Dyer. After a pause, she changed her mind saying, "OK, I work for you."

Lt. Hollar's uniform at the 199th LIB

There was a swimming pool, PX, and air-conditioned library within a five-minute walk from my room. The Officer's Club was very nice and served everything from hamburgers to steak dinner. The hamburgers and French fries reminded me of McDonald's. Sometimes there would be a cookout where we grilled our steak, spare ribs, or chicken. My assignment differed drastically from being an infantry platoon leader and was infinitely safer.

Major Byrd, the S-1, was often assigned special projects I would complete. For Armed Forces Day in May, I was tasked with writing a statement for the brigade commander to be sent to all personnel in the brigade. The theme of my letter was to say how great a job everyone was doing.

In 2011 I began counseling with a therapist for Post Traumatic Stress Disorder (PTSD) and depression. My therapist once asked me how I adjusted to such a change. I had not thought of that before. I hesitated and replied, "I just changed caps." That seems to be a requirement for officers in the military. They need to adjust and quickly change caps. The training at OCS helped prepare me to do just that.

Captain Wise was my immediate supervisor, and he was scheduled to DEROS (Date of Estimated Return from Overseas) in May. I was involved in auditing and reviewing several monetary funds in the brigade. The Brigade Commander was General Bond. I would see those things he wanted to be made, such as plaques, silver-coated pistols, etc., as gifts for various officers leaving the 199th.

On March 25, I completed the Army form that was used to request my next (and final) assignment. The assistant S-1, Captain Juran, suggested I ask where I could use my accounting major. Therefore, my first choice was the Pentagon. Other choices included Forts Belvoir, Myer, Eustis, Monroe, and Lee, all in Virginia.

One trip to Saigon involved buying felt to line a box in which a plaque would be placed. One time, I needed 10 sets of Signal Corp Officer Insignia plaques. The PX was out, so I wrote Sylvia to see if she could find them at Fort Myer or Cameron Station. As it turned out, I was able to find them in Saigon. Sylvia was my assistant, even being 10,000 miles away. I called her on the MARS line to tell her that she did not need to look for them. The MARS station at the 199th was much nicer than at Dau Tieng. There was a private booth for making calls, and it was air-conditioned. At the end of May, the building that housed the S-1 office was also air-conditioned. That starkly contrasted my time in the jungle with the First Infantry Division.

In a letter from Sylvia, she expressed disappointment in what the protesters were doing in the States. I replied: "I'm in full sympathy with your thoughts on the protestors." In later years I realized that they helped accelerate the end of the war. "Everything they want will eventually result from what is done in Cambodia. They want the war to end now, not just because they hate killing but mainly because THEY don't want to come here. It is a rare luxury for any generation to avoid a war. They seem least able to face it until they get here, but they turn out to be some outstanding guys once they're here. Still, they hate killing - but they hate dying even more."

Since I was making plaques for work, I decided to make ones for my mother and Sylvia for Mother's Day. Both enjoyed and appreciated them.

Saigon is a busy place. A zillion motor scooters were buzzing around. It is a wonder the drivers did not kill themselves. In a tape, I described it as "a desperate place" regarding its traffic. It is a Vietnamese custom for everything to close from noon to 3 pm. Traffic stopped, stores closed their doors, and street vendors stopped selling.

In an April 2 letter to the church, I wrote:

"When seeing the President's Palace in Saigon, it is evident that this is a country at war. Inside the iron fence around the grounds, every 75 feet is built a bunker of sandbags. There is also barb wire circling the fence. There are periodic locations where ARVN soldiers are on guard with a 50-caliber machine gun mounted.

"Downtown, however, except for seeing soldiers here and there, you would never know a war was going on anywhere. There are many, many Honda scooters over here. For every car, there must be 20 scooters. People drive anywhere, anyway, anytime. At intersections, there are no left-turn lights. You turn left, right, around, or whatever you can. Today I saw a car and scooter parked in the middle of the street of a Saigon suburb with the two drivers talking on the sidewalk. This would be like parking your car in front of the Falls Church bank on the center dividing line and going to lunch. Hostile fire pay is well earned just driving in Saigon. DC rush hour is heavenly calm compared to here."

I performed "staff studies," which meant reviewing reports summarizing their content before forwarding them to General Bond. Major Bell, the S-1, would review them before forwarding them to the General. Sometimes, they were dull, like the one investigating inventory variances at the Brigade Post Exchange store.

On March 29, I wrote to Sylvia, "Out in the field, I had a problem of what to write every three days. I mean, after all, what was there to say? We went four clicks – killed two – it was hot – no one hurt today. You just don't write stuff like that to your wife."

In a May 31 letter to Sylvia, I wrote:

"This week an air conditioner was installed in our office. ROUGH WAR? Regardless of what advantages one has, complaints always abound - it's not cool enough. During my first six months, I could not have imagined a place existing like this in the whole of Vietnam. Actually, only about 50,000 out of the 500,000 here are infantry[18] out in the jungle. Many have a comfortable life. The contrast between the majority in secure locations and the lonely infantryman in the jungle is impossible to describe.

The other day I escorted two new captains to Xuan Loc, the forward operating base, to be interviewed by the brigade commander. We went the 40 miles by jeep and saw the countryside and some villages. The road was paved with all kinds of motorbikes, trucks, and other vehicles. Along the way were a number of rice fields and rubber plantations with Vietnamese workers busy. It was about an hour's ride. On a trip like that, the only weapons I carried were a pistol, and the driver had an M-16 rifle. The road was entirely secure and heavily traveled.

On April 1, General Bond, the brigade commander, was killed while in the field. Of course, this was a big shock to everyone. Generals are not exempt from the threat of death in combat. A memorial service was held on April 3. Fifty or sixty generals attended, along with General Abrams and Ambassador Bunker. The general had the habit of landing on the ground when there was contact. He was killed by a single bullet that likely came from a sniper. He should not have been on the ground during a battle.

The S-1 office was tasked with planning the memorial service. It involved a lot of coordination and communication with others. I was tasked with preparing a memorial package for his wife. One desk in our office was manned by one of the enlisted men. It had three or four phones on it. He was getting a lot of calls because of the memorial service. The two captains in the office and I decided that we would simultaneously place a call to three of the phones. The guy

---

[18] In any major military operation, no more than 10% of the total number of troops are in the infantry. Only about 9% of the officers in the army have infantry as their military occupation specialty (MOS).

at the desk almost went berserk, with all three ringing. We all had a good laugh out of it.

On April 4, I took a chopper to one of the brigade firebases at Xuan Loc. Sometimes I would go by jeep. It was a 50-minute trip on a well-traveled and safe road. I needed to deliver several plaques. I had been issued a flak jacket, and I wore it to the base and was armed with a .45 caliber pistol. It seemed strange to have a flak jacket when it was hardly needed. It would have been helpful in the field, although it would have been too heavy and hot for comfort. In a letter that night to Sylvia, I commented, "It's marvelous – I have fresh clothes every morning to wear and a shower every day."

On another occasion, I traveled to Xuan Loc via helicopter to deliver several plaques. The pilot decided it was "playtime" and swooped up and down, coming within 50 feet of the ground. That did not help my blood pressure or stomach.

My hours at the S-1 office were 8 am to 5 pm daily. I had enough work to keep me busy for six hours, and I was on call 24 hours a day. I would take breaks during the day. In a tape to my wife, I said: "The Army does many stupid things, which is one of the reasons I will not be staying in."

On Sunday, April 5, I was able to go to the chapel service at 9 am. Captain Jiran suggested I take the afternoon off, so I went to the library, read, and relaxed. That evening I went to the Officer's Club and met several guys who were with me at the 95th Officer Candidate Company. We determined who we knew of from the 95th that had been killed in Vietnam. Ray Long was one of them. In my letter to Sylvia that evening, I wrote:

"Ray Long was killed in Delta company in November. I didn't want to tell you about it at the time while I was still out. He is the only person I knew well to have been lost there. I remember I found out while the company was at the airstrip waiting to go on our three-day stand down at Dian, the First Division headquarters. It was quite a shock, especially after talking with him just a few weeks earlier. Ray was the only officer in the battalion killed while I was there."

Once, I wrote to Sylvia that, "Everything I ever told you about the field was true (except possibly once). I just didn't always tell you everything. I wrote Paul about most of the contact we had, but no one else. It is different from an older brother. Only once did we run into anything horrible, and that was October 2. I mentioned it to you around the 4th but only casually as 'nothing much.' I may tell you some about it later. That was the only time the company lost anyone due to enemy action while I was there.

"I know of some people whose parents don't even know they're in Vietnam – they think they are in Thailand. I couldn't see going that far. I always told you the truth – on some matters, not the whole truth, and often nothing.

"It was rough writing home. It would often take 30 minutes for a small page. A letter becomes a strain when your everyday experiences are contrary to acceptable correspondence to your mother or father. Once, I remember, after 15 minutes and only two sentences, I closed with 'I can't think of anything to say' and signed it."

In a letter from my mother, she wrote: "You are no better off at the 199th than anywhere else." I considered myself to be completely safe in my new assignment. I spent 10 minutes explaining how secure I was compared to being in the jungle on a tape to Sylvia. However, the fact that our general had been killed in combat did not reduce her fears.

The frustration of being there came out. I wrote to Sylvia: "The more I think about it, the people back home have no conception in any way, shape, or form of what is even happening here or what it's like at all. They have no basis for making any judgments about the war."

I also saw Major Stemsley at the base. He was the Executive Officer of my basic training battalion at Fort Benning when I was a training officer. I was standing outside the door to the S-1 and saw him headed for the S-4 office. He was a battalion commander of the 18th ARVN Division, serving as an advisor.

My military pay at the time consisted of a Base Pay of $534, Quarters, $120, Subsistence, $47, and Combat Pay, $65. My deductions included taxes, a bond, meals, and an allotment to Sylvia of $500. That left me with $190 cash to buy burgers, steak, and fries at the club.

In a letter to Sylvia, I wrote:

"I'm in the office now, and it's just beginning to build up to a storm outside. Off in the distance across Long Binh Post can be seen clouds of dust being swept up. The military complex has cleared large areas leaving dust free to roam. The rain is off to the east, coming from the ocean. The monsoon season may be ushered in today.

"I don't know if I can bear the other 92 days here. It seems so close yet so very far away. With everyone demonstrating and worse – why bother? Sometimes it all seems so futile, so wasted, and everyone else seems to think so too. It's just so long to August.

"If anybody thinks I'm coming back home and lift a rifle against Ohio State, Kent State, Augusta, Georgia, or anywhere else, they are sadly mistaken. I hope I'm never asked because I'm unsure what my answer might be."

While at the 199th, I had opportunities to purchase items from the PACEX (Army and Air Force Pacific Exchange Service) catalog. It included many electronic and camera items. Prices were half what they would cost in the States, so most GIs bought things. Since the prices were so reasonable, purchasing stuff became a disease. I got a Minolta camera and stereo equipment. I also purchased cameras for my parents and Sylvia's parents. I asked my brother, Paul, if he wanted anything. He replied that he did but was hesitant to ask me, considering what I had to go through to buy in Vietnam. I did write a letter to Sylvia where I told her I would ONLY purchase things for their family and us. I said the cost of having to come here was too high. If our friends want something from here, they would have to wait until their son is sent here because it costs more than dollars to make purchases here.

On May 1, under orders from President Nixon, elements of the First Calvary Division, 25th Infantry Division, and the 11th Armored Calvary units entered Cambodia in the "Parrot's Beak" to deter the NVA's ability to attack inside Vietnam. The 199th Division assisted in the operation with two of its four battalions securing the First Cav's firebases east of the Cambodia border. Also, some 15,000 ARVN troops participated in the invasion.

May 1 was May Day for the communist world. It seemed like Tet in reverse to me. In a May 1, 1970 letter to my pastor and church members, I wrote: "You think you are surprised at the invasion; how do you think Joe Private in the 1st Air Calvary Division feels? Surprise is not the word for him. Terrified is closer to the truth."

I detailed my thoughts to church members in a May 1 letter:

"If you are confused about what is happening over here, then join the crowd. President Nixon may be the only one who knows. You think you are surprised; how do you think Joe Private in the 1st Air Calvary Division doing the job feels? Surprised is not the word for him. TERRIFIED is closer.

"Before becoming all aroused, stop and think how Americans felt here with the NVA (well trained, well equipped, and well supplied) 30 miles from Saigon, utterly safe for the last five years. The men here are going to sleep a little better when this operation is completed. It is long overdue - by about four years.

"Elements of the 25th Infantry Division, the 1st Air Cavalry Division, the 11th Armored Cavalry Regiment, and some 15,000 ARVN troops are massing the attack. If you want to put your prayers and thoughts where they count, direct them towards those young captains, lieutenants, sergeants, and privates who must pay the high price. Life for them will have a flavor the protected will never have to know.

"I'm sure there are some bewildering faces among the NVA soldiers along the Cambodian border. It might do well to remember that the cost will be so high for the North Vietnamese soldiers caught there. I am sure they do not know 'what's happening, for the most part. The actual cause of the war is sealed safely somewhere in Hanoi. The young NVA soldier loses—seeing him in that light while out in the jungle is difficult. He also has a mind, heart, wife, or girlfriend, and the capacity for human love. The greatest tragedy of this war (and all wars) is that the men behind it all will never suffer any loss, and justice will never be brought to bear on them - at least not in this life. They also have a sanctuary in which to hide.

"This war has cost one President to be a one-term Commander in Chief. Johnson was wise enough to leave the office before the votes were cast. Nixon may be faced with the same future. War always has cost so much for so many.

"In my first letter to you last October, I made a statement that I firmly believe.[19] How the President handles this war, and Vietnamization will significantly influence how world history is recorded for the next 25 or 50 years."

On May 2, I wrote, "Senator Kennedy calls the current operation madness. I call the current operation of college students madness."

At 6:30 am on May 3, the II Field Force siren went off, indicating incoming rockets. It was a half-mile from my location. It was quite a sight to see all the GIs from the barracks outside in their shorts wearing flak jackets.

On May 8, I became a "two-digit midget". That meant that the number of days before my DEROS could be counted with two digits – 99. It was a significant accomplishment for any soldier there. From then on, I would write my number of days to DEROS on almost every letter I sent to Sylvia.

Cameras and stereo equipment made in Japan could be bought in Vietnam for about half the cost in the States. Sylvia and I exchanged many letters and tapes discussing what we should buy. We ordered several pieces of stereo equipment which we have to this day. I also ordered several cameras. On May 9, I received a letter from the Saigon Postal Authorities saying that the Minolta camera I ordered was stolen. The box had been broken open, and the camera was gone. Fortunately, I had insured the order, so the camera was replaced at no additional cost. I filed a claim on May 10 for $131. I was told it would take one to three months to receive a refund.

On a recent Paul Harvey show, I heard that Bob Jones Jr. said the four at Kent University got what they deserved. I

---

[19] Decades later I realize that my statement is still true. However, the impact of losing an unnecessary war gives me pause to consider how things might have been.

am below judging the justice of death. It is a tragic loss under any circumstances. However, the stuff the kids are doing almost inevitably points toward disaster – and it came. This week's toll from the war will be in the hundreds here and four in the United States.

I began recording a taped diary on November 28. At one point, I said: "I am getting tired of everything here, and over 200 days left seems like a heck of a long time. It all gets to be old, even ancient."

The first thing I discussed in the diary was the friendly fire event described in Chapter 12. In the entire journal, I did not speak of the October 2 battle. I believe it was too fresh in my mind, and I did not want to say the words aloud. Before talking about the October 31 encounter with a man on a trail, I noted that I was smoking a Dutch Panatela cigar just for kicks. I said I would not try cigarettes because I did not want to get addicted. On the tape, I said: "Maybe I need the cigar. I'm beginning to get a little edgy over here."

Sgt. Ken Tucker from Mike Platoon came by one evening. It was good to visit with him. He was on his way to Sydney on R&R. I recall that he was an excellent platoon sergeant.

In January 1970, Mike Timma arrived in South Vietnam. We graduated together from Bob Jones University in May 1967 with majors in accounting. He was drafted into the Army after receiving a Master of Business Administration from the University of Florida. He was assigned to the 1st Logistical Command in Finance at Long Binh. Later he was assigned to the Army & Air Force Exchange Service in Cholon, a community within Saigon. His duties included seeking reconciliation and collection of delinquent accounts. I expected that having auditing experience in Atlanta, a bachelor's degree in accounting, and an MBA assisted by being assigned to the finance area. In addition to a visit, we spoke on the phone a few times.

Saigon was about 17 miles north of the 199th base camp, so on June 6, he came for a visit. He had half a day on Saturday and all day off on Sunday. He slept in one of the empty rooms of our building. We had dinner at a Chinese restaurant on Long Binh Post Saturday evening. We visited late into Saturday night. I got to sleep around midnight. He wanted me to visit his place in Saigon sometime and see the city. I told him that it was unlikely that I would be willing to leave the base overnight.

He left Sunday morning for Saigon. He hitchhiked back, planning to catch a ride on an Army vehicle. That was the acceptable way to get around.

Periodically a practice red alert was done. When that happens, reassigned personnel are to go to the bunkers on the base perimeter. My job was to inspect to see if my assigned people did what the procedures required. I found that almost everyone was where they should have been.

In June, the S-1 section set up a volleyball court near the office. Groups of us would play for an hour or two. It was good exercise and would help burn some calories the chow hall food put on. I realized I could get a free subscription to *The Chicago Tribune*. I would receive it about a week after the publication date. I wrote Sylvia, "...it's probably the most conservative newspaper in the States. Balancing its conservatism with *The Washington Post* and *New York Times* would yield a picture of both sides, which I am coming to think more and more is where the answers most likely lie."

At the end of May, I received my orders for my next assignment. It would be at Ft. Mead, Maryland. I received a letter from a major at the fort telling me that a lieutenant was appointed as my sponsor. My replacement at the 199th would be Lt. Jim Sussman, and I would be training him during my last month. He also spent two weeks at the forward operating base at Xuan Loc. I had Jim take over things on August 1. I wrote Sylvia after that, "I probably won't be around much at all. I don't know where I'll go, however."

I wrote a letter to President Nixon late in May, saying, "Thanks for watching out for us." I received a reply thanking me for my service here. I thought my letter was more potent than a university demonstration.

One day Jim, another lieutenant (Larry Lozowski), and I went to Saigon. Jim had an address of a band that played at the officer's club, so he wanted to see them - for the girls, of course. There were three dancers/singers from the Philippines, and both Jim and the other lieutenant wished to take them to the ISO club for cokes, which we did. One of them said they liked playing for GIs because it made them feel good and happy. Larry planned to return on Saturday and take all three to the officer's club at Thon Son Nhut for dinner.

Major Bell was the nervous type, and almost everyone in the office did not like him. Looking back, I expect he was having some PTSD issues from earlier assignments in combat. When I went to Xuan Loc, one of the sergeants there told me that Colonel Shelton, the Brigade Commander, told him "to keep an eye on Major Bell." When he left at the end of May, no one gave him a gift, although we gave gifts to a clerk and Captain Wise. The office referred to him as "ding-dong." I hope I refrained from that.

Major Volponi replaced Major Bell in June. He was a vast improvement, and everyone liked him very much. We learned that the 199th would be withdrawn with the October 15 redeployments at the end of June. An early indicator that the brigade would be leaving was that a colonel would be replacing General Bond. Otherwise, a general would have been assigned. Also, the long delay in appointing a replacement for General Bond was an indicator that something was up.

Major Volponi asked Jim and me whether we would extend our tours until the redeployment was accomplished. He said, however, that he would not ask anyone to do that, knowing that if it were him, even as a career man, he would be on the plane on "his" day unless there were a desirable offer. I was honored that he wanted me to stay but respectfully declined the offer. When I left for home, Major Tony Volponi asked me to get some of the "Tony the Tiger" material and send it to him. That was the mascot for Kellogg's Frosted Flakes and was trendy back home. I did do that for him.

There was one point in the President's withdrawal plan that was not literally kept. It was his reference to the number of troops being "withdrawn." In reality, few or no troops came home. It was the number of new soldiers coming. That number was reduced, and those who DEROS were not replaced. Those high school students who benefitted were the ones who graduated in 1969 and later. Those of us who graduated before 1969 were the losers.

While at the 199th, I signed up for a photography class. Since I had ordered a Minolta camera, I thought it would be helpful. No one else did because almost everyone dropped out after the first class, and the class was canceled.

On July 18, Colonel Selton would be leaving Vietnam. The Deputy Commanding Officer, Colonel Hendry, would be taking over command. There was a "big" change of command ceremony, which the S-1 office was responsible for organizing. One of the items needed was invitations and programs for the ceremony. Another lieutenant and I went to Saigon on June 30 and ordered them. On July 7, we had the invitations and began distributing them.

The First Air Calvary Division General Casey was killed in a chopper crash on July 12. Colonel Hendry was with him in the chopper and was flown to a hospital in Japan. A few days later, we learned that Colonel Collins would take over the brigade and that the change of command ceremony would proceed on the 18th.

By early July, my mind was on only one thing – going home. On July 24, I wrote Sylvia: "I went and saw *The Arrangement* tonight but left after the second reel because it required mental attention, which I have not had for 30 days."

When I had only about three weeks before going home, I reflected on the year and what it would be like going home. I concluded that going home would be such a catastrophic change that I could not imagine how it would be. I had so little in common with many of the people I saw there.

On July 28, a ceremony was held to present the Distinguished Service Cross to a sergeant. It was for his actions when his platoon position was attacked at night. General Robson, the deputy commanding general of US forces in Vietnam, presented the award. It was an impressive ceremony.

Sylvia and I exchanged several letters discussing where we would stay immediately upon my return. She had an apartment ready near Ft. Meade, my next assignment. At first, I suggested that we stay at my parents' home for several days and then go to the apartment in Laurel, Maryland. When Sylvia told my parents we would stay at the apartment when we first got home, confusion ensued. However, I had written a letter to them saying we would stay with them for the first few days.

I wrote a clarification letter stating that I was wrong and Sylvia was right. I ended the message with: "We'll celebrate out of our base camp at Laurel and be sending frequent search and clear missions and patrols out across the Potomac."

It was difficult communicating via letters since it took eight to 10 days for a round-trip exchange. After exchanging more letters, we decided to stay at the apartment for a few days with my parents. Her parents lived nearby.

One day, during lunch, I lay in the sun for 50 minutes, hoping to get a tan before going home. I wrote Sylvia: "I haven't been that uncomfortable since being in the jungle. In the future, I will lay out by the pool so I can cool off when needed by taking a dip."

Six guys I knew on one Saturday in July went to Vung Tau for the weekend. It was a 50-mile trip and spot for in-country R&R on the ocean. I had planned to join them until the night before when we were at the officer's club. They were all getting drunk and began making standard drunken comments about the girls (prostitution organized by Uncle Sam) they expected to find and how drunk they would get. That exchange convinced me to ignore their knock on my door at 6 am.

Also, we had planned to go in the daily military police-escorted convoy. They decided to go to the officer's club on their own and bring their weapons. That included a machine gun and M16s. The likelihood of them being attacked on the route was 1,000 to one against it. However, it only takes one bullet, and I had far more than enough risk-taking in the jungle when I had nothing to say about it. I had everything to say about it, which stacked the cards in my favor. And, of course, I did not want to become another Casualty of War.

In July, I received a letter from Dave Ellis, the office manager of the Washington office of Arthur Andersen & Co. I had sent him a letter asking various questions about my reemployment. One question regarded when hospitalization insurance would begin. He said the hospitalization would be effective when I started work, but for maternity benefits, pregnancy would have to have occurred after starting work.

In a letter to Sylvia, I wrote:

"Do you realize that every commercial on TV will be new to me when I get home? Most of the shows, half of the growing DC area, all of the radio ads, all of the local news, all of the styles over the last 12 months, all of the new cars, all of the higher prices, everyone will be a year older, many are against the effort here, and everything will be DIFFICULT. If I wore a uniform, I could be shot as quickly in the US as in Saigon. Everyone in the US wants the war to end, but no one wants to come and complete it."

In a tape letter to Sylvia, I described what I felt about the differences between my assignment at the 199th and when I was a platoon leader:

"The main difference in my responsibilities now is that if I do something wrong at S-1, the only thing that will happen is that a bunch of captains, majors, or colonels will get mad and give me a bad report which will, in reality, amount to nothing. However, if I made a colossal mistake in the field as a platoon leader, not only would captains, majors, and a colonel get teed off, and I would be relieved of duty, but, and this is my biggest fear, it could result in the loss of someone's life, or someone's arm, eye, or leg.

"I am thankful that nothing of this sort ever happened to me. I have no second thoughts about any actions I took. As far as I know, nothing that I did was directly related to harm coming to anyone else. This, in my mind, is the final evaluation.

"The people I'll never forget will be those I worked with in my platoon. I'll remember them most in the times when the chips were down."

20

Welcome Home?

"A time comes when silence is betrayal."
- Dr. Martin Luther King

On Veterans Day 2010, Vietnam veterans Bill White and Jim Ryon were reunited in Washington, DC after four decades. "In those days, they had been 20-year-old sailors, heaving powder and shell into a five-inch gun amid smoke and noise of the number-two mount as USS Storms plastered the coast of Vietnam in September 1966."[20] When they met at Reagan National Airport, Ryon said to Bill, "*Welcome home*, brother."

In 2007 Don Meyer sent me a copy of his Vietnam War memoir, *The Protected Will Never Know*. He signed the first page: "To Dave! *Welcome Home!* Best Wishes, Don Meyer, 3/12/2007." Thirty-seven years after I returned home, he still felt it proper to welcome me. The lack of positive reception from America was a slap in the face that had not healed.

The dedication of the Vietnam Veterans Memorial was on Veterans Day in 1982. Across the Washington Mall, a constant echo of "*Welcome Home, Welcome Home, Welcome Home*" came from the Vietnam veterans as they greeted each other after 20 years of neglect.

---

[20] Michael E. Ruane. "For Former Shipmates, Some Memories Never Fade." *The Washington Post*, 12 November 2010, sec B, p.1.

Sylvia expected me to arrive home on August 16 or 17. I had been able to catch a flight out of Bien Hoa Air Base a day early. Dennis King was on my flight. He had lost 20% of his hearing on October 2 but had recovered from his other wounds. He served his last months as an aide to a general. I suffered hearing loss mainly in my right ear since I am right-handed, and my rifle would be at that ear when I fired it.

As the jetliner began taxiing down the runway, I could not help but think of the sequence of events over the next few minutes. I mentally clicked off the steps as we soared into the sky out of harm's way.

The instant the wheels lifted off the runway, my count began. It was all my estimations, but I thought them to be accurate. The first 30 seconds after liftoff, we were out of small arms range. A grenade tossed towards the aircraft would fall short of its target. In 40 seconds, Charlie's AK-47 could no longer harm me. Another 25 seconds passed, and we had escaped the range of his RPG launchers.

My FREEDOM BIRD was soaring into the bright blue sky over the Republic of South Vietnam. I was now SAFE unless the plane crashed.

When we came home from Vietnam, we were expected to become once again law-abiding, distinguished citizens of our country. Hours earlier, we left a country where death, dismemberment, and destruction were the accepted norms. There was no counseling or instruction on becoming one of the millions of citizens going about their daily activities in our respective communities.

We were expected to present briefings to the corporate board of directors on how the new product line was doing in the western region. We were expected to deliver the 500 cases of cola to the stores on our delivery route. We were expected to nail a thousand nails each day as we constructed new homes for American families. We were expected to dig ditches, wash dishes, wait tables, draw tattoos, preach sermons, teach students, prepare tax returns and Security and Exchange (SEC) K-1 statements, and tend to thousands of other occupations and professions as we blended into our communities.

No one warned us that there would be flashbacks, nightmares, and posttraumatic stress to greet us with our return to "The World." No one told us of the impending diseases caused by exposure to Agent Orange. Few understood where we had been, what we had done, the things we had seen, touched, and smelled, or why we were there. Few understood why we went to 'Nam in the first place. Even fewer wanted to know. Unless we had an understanding family, we were on our own. Some did not make it. I did.

The flight from Vietnam to home was 19 hours -- just like the flight I made in September 1969 to 'Nam. This time, however, it seemed like a 50-hour flight. We stopped in Guam to refuel. I bought a much-anticipated grilled ham and cheese sandwich with a cold, cold Coke. It could not have tasted better.

I was on my way to McGuire Air Force Base in New Jersey after a brief stop in Alaska. I muddled through the paperwork and caught the first taxi to the Philadelphia airport. I bought a ticket to Washington, DC, and called Sylvia.

Her surprise at my early arrival was very apparent.

"I'm not ready," she exclaimed. She had more to do with getting our apartment ready.

Sylvia, her sister Judy, and her mother had been preparing our apartment near Ft. Meade. They had just finished the day before. I told her I would arrive at National Airport in a few hours. Of course, that meant nothing to me - I was home, and that was that.

When my plane took off from the Philadelphia airport, I did not count the seconds or think about danger. I was home. I was in the United States of America, and I was safe – unless the plane crashed. However, I was still a Casualty of War.

Upon disembarking from the plane, my eyes feasted on the most beautiful face on the planet. We embraced, kissed, and shed tears of joy.

Sylvia had debated calling my parents and telling them of my arrival or surprising them with us coming to their home. She did the "unselfish" thing, and they were at the airport. The reunion was one I will not forget.

We went directly to our new apartment in Laurel, Maryland. It was decorated beautifully. I was so happy to be home. After a while, Mom and Dad mentioned that they should call a cab to get home, knowing that we probably had some "personal things" to attend to. Of course, that would not do, so we drove them back to Fairfax, VA - about a 50-mile one-way journey. That evening Sylvia and I returned to the apartment. We went to bed and arose very late the following day.

The following Sunday, we went to our home church's morning and evening services, at National Gardens Baptist, in Falls Church, VA. I was considering many in the States' attitudes about the war and chose not to wear my uniform. It was sad that I felt that way.

After the evening service, the congregation would gather in the fellowship hall for coffee, juice, and cookies and "fellowshipped" with each other. As we went down the steps toward the entrance, I said to Sylvia, "Let's just go on home now."

Considering how long we had been apart, I may have had some ideas for the evening. After all, it was over an hour's drive to the apartment, and it was already 8:30 in the evening. Sylvia insisted that we go to the hall, so I reluctantly agreed.

A large "Welcome Home Dave" banner was hanging from the ceiling as we entered the room. It was a tremendous welcoming, which I remember to this day.

It was also the last such banner I would see for a dozen years. Over the next decade, I made little mention of my year in Vietnam, where I was, what I did, or what I thought of it. No one wanted to hear about it. Therefore, I remained silent. Silence can be an evil partner. Having done what I did and saw what I saw, the silence was not a healing device. It was the opposite.

Vietnam veterans needed to "step out of the darkness upon our return." William Mahedy captured these thoughts and feelings in *Out of the Night - The Spiritual Journey of*

Vietnam Vets. It was published in 1986 and reissued in paperback in 2007. Mahedy, an Episcopal priest, served as a chaplain in Vietnam. He helped develop the Vietnam Vet Centers Program at the Department of Veterans Affairs. His book is a powerful presentation of the demons that sought to destroy Vietnam veterans. They have succeeded in doing so all too often. I posted the following review of the paperback on February 11, 2008.

> "I read the first edition of "Out of the Night" about 16 years after returning from South Vietnam where I served an infantry platoon leader with the First Infantry Division. It is a compelling work that will help the Veteran come "out of the night" and other readers better understand what happened there and what happened to the men and women who served there.
>
> "The Vietnam War was the defining event of my adult life. Its impact was tremendous and intense. William Mahedy captures the thoughts and fears of many Veterans.
>
> "Martin Luther King was right when he said ""A time comes when silence is betrayal." Mahedy was not silent and many have benefited."

I read Mahedy's book in 1986 when it was first published. As a Vietnam veteran who served in combat, I could relate to his analysis of us and the thinking of other vets he quotes in the book. When I arrived in Vietnam, I was convinced that the war was the "noble cause" President Reagan later proclaimed it to be.

After returning home, I realized that it was nothing of the kind; it was a "National Nightmare" void of any redemptive value.

A five-day "National Salute to Vietnam Veterans" was held on November 10-14, 1982. It was when the Vietnam Veterans Memorial on the Washington Mall was dedicated. The memorial was the idea and dream of Jan C. Scruggs, who served in Vietnam with the 199th Light Infantry Brigade. He was 19 when he went to Vietnam right after graduating from Bowie High School in Maryland.

A candlelight vigil was held at the National Cathedral beginning Wednesday, November 10, and continued as the 58,000 names of those killed in Vietnam were read aloud. The readings concluded on Friday, November 12, around midnight – for a total of 56 hours. Volunteers read the names. I went to the cathedral during some of the reading of names. It was a solemn and reflective time of remembrance.

The climax of the five days was a parade and the memorial's dedication on Saturday, November 13. Sylvia, Mike, and I attended the events on that day.

The "parades featured large formations of Vietnam veterans, marching by state, supported by bands, floats, active-duty military units, and various groups. The parade includes disabled Vietnam veterans, massed colors, and 25 Grand Marshals drawn from the ranks of Vietnam veterans in sports and show business, government, Vietnam Medal of Honor winners, and ranking officers and enlisted Vietnam veterans still on active duty. It was estimated that 205,000 veterans, their families, and other observers attended the parade. At noon US Air Force and US Navy F-4s and US Army helicopters flew down Independence Avenue to honor the veterans."[21]

The three of us attended the 1:00 p.m. memorial service at the First Division Memorial at 17th street and State Place, just one block from the General Services Administration building where I worked. The monument honors the 12,000 men of the Big Red One who lost their lives in three wars. The Vietnam wing of the memorial was the first significant national tribute erected to Vietnam veterans. The service was moving.

Dedication to the memorial began at 2:00 p.m. Maya Ying Lin designed the monument. Her design was selected from the 1,421 submissions. There was opposition to the design. Major objections were that it was black, the color of defeat, sunken into the ground like a hole. From the beginning, I liked the design. I thought having the names inscribed was an honor to them.

---

[21] *The Washington Post*. I do not recall the exact reference.

I recall being very disappointed at the timing of the death of Leonid Brezhnev, President of the Soviet Union, on November 10, 1982. His death was the primary news subject for days, overshadowing coverage of the parade and memorial dedication. It was on the front page of every newspaper. *Newsweek*'s November 22, 1982 issues had a photo of the Soviet Union's new head, Yuri Andropov, on the cover. A small headline at the top of the page read, "Honoring Our Vietnam Veterans – At Last." The November 22 issue of *US News & World Report* featured Brezhnev on the cover, and a story about the veterans' activities was buried on page 66. It figured; that even when we were to get our due, a USSR leader's death usurped our story. That was par for the course.

One event of the week was the hopeful reunion of fellow soldiers that served in one's unit. The First Infantry Division had its reunion headquarters in the Washington Sheraton Hotel. One evening I went to the hotel, hoping to find someone I knew while I was in Vietnam. I searched the lists provided and everyone who had signed in but to no avail. It was highly disappointing not to be connected with anyone who was there with me. It was a disappointment in a week of celebration.

The cover of *Newsweek*'s special issue on December 14, 1981, read "What Vietnam Did to Us." It tells the story of 54 men in Charlie Company of the First Infantry Division's Second Battalion of the 28th Infantry Regiment in Vietnam in 1968-69. This may have been the first time a national magazine dealt with the subject of Vietnam. The issue spelled out the feelings of most Vietnam veterans when it said:

> "...the million men who served in combat in the longest war America has ever fought and the only war it has ever lost. There were no rites of coronation at their homecoming, no brass bands or crowds cheering at the docks or celebratory rhetoric floating across the village greens. The veterans of the defeated US mission in Vietnam returned instead to a kind of embarrassed silence, *as if,* one of them thought, *everyone was ashamed of us.* They have been obliged to bear an inordinate share of the blame for having fought at all and for having failed to win. Some have

paid a terrible further cost in stunted careers, shattered marriages, and disfigured lives. Yet most have endured with a stubborn hardihood, a living reminder in our midst of a war that never really ended for them or their countrymen."[22]

In 1995 former Secretary of Defense Robert S. McNamara said that we should have withdrawn from South Vietnam in late 1963.

For years, the American people were disenchanted. As a veteran of the Vietnam War, it would be easy for me to be disappointed with my service. However, I answered my nation's call to serve and fight for what we had been told was a noble cause. Indeed, it may have been noble initially, but, over time and with the loss of thousands and thousands of America's bests, it became a national nightmare. We soon learned that there was no light at the end of the tunnel.

We, the soldiers who fought the war, retain our honor for serving when called – and for the most part, did so without protest. In the end, it is Robert S. McNamara who redeemed us.

In a January 1970 tape to Sylvia, I said:

"The Army messed up regarding keeping me in the Army. They messed up from the very beginning. If the recruiters had told me the truth and they had told me the right thing all along, then the Army might have had a chance of keeping me. There is no chance now in a hundred years, especially since my college major was accounting and the chance of getting into the Finance Corps is slim."

In addition to not receiving a Welcome Home, we were at a clear disadvantage regarding actually winning the war.

The maximum U.S. troop level in South Vietnam during the war was 543,400[23] in April 1969, five months before I went there. However, in June, President Nixon began withdrawing the first 25,000 troops.

---

[22] Peter Goldman, "What Vietnam Did to Us," *Newsweek*, December, 14 1981.
[23] https://www.vietnamwar50th.com/history_and_legacy/timeline/

We have since learned that it was not enough to accomplish the mission in South Vietnam - to prevent North Vietnam from overtaking the south. Not nearly enough. To make matters worse, that was known by U.S. high officials as early as 1966.

In the 1980s, Emeritus Professor Mark Stoler of the University of Vermont spent a year teaching at the Office of Strategic Studies at the Naval War College. He learned there that the number needed was two million troops. He later heard the same number from other sources.

A history professor at the University of Houston told me that after the Tet Offensive in February 1968, General Wheeler, the Chairman of the Joint Chiefs of Staff, told President Johnson that an additional 500,000 troops were needed. At that time, there were already 500,000 US troops in South Vietnam.

In 1966 high military officers were saying that one million troops were needed. There were about 250,000 troops there at that time.

In March 1968, General Westmorland requested an additional 206,000[24] troops to augment the 500,000 already in South Vietnam.

The American people would NEVER have accepted the level of commitment and the number of dead soldiers that would have resulted if we were to accomplish our mission - to win the war and keep South Vietnam an independent country.

Ronald Reagan said the war was a "noble cause." It was a "National Nightmare." All military and civilian personnel sent there were "set up" to fail.

---

[24] https://www.vietnamwar50th.com/1968_tet_and_shifting_views/The-New-York-Times-Reports-that-General-William-C-Westmoreland-has-Requested-206-000-Additional-Troops/

21

Dying for Your Country

"My job is not to die for my country; It's to see how many of those bastards I can kill for their country."[25]
- Command Sgt. Maj. Michael McCoy, before deploying for Iraq

In 1969, the movie *The Green Berets* was released. Sylvia and I saw it at a theatre in Fort Benning, Georgia. I recall being impressed by it, which further convinced me that our cause in Vietnam was just and right. I saw it on television again in 2007. One of the early scenes is when an Army sergeant is lecturing to a group of journalists and ordinary Americans. One of the journalists, George Beckworth (played by David Jansen), tells the sergeant that it "seems like this is a war between the Vietnamese people. Let them handle it." Beckman's newspaper opposes the war. The sergeant then lists various weapons the NVA and Viet Cong soldiers used as coming from Red China, Chinese communists, Russian communists, and Czechoslovakian communists. He then proclaims, "What is involved here is communist domination of the world." While this is happening, Colonel Mike Kirby (John Wayne) is looking on approvingly at the sergeant's response.

---

[25] Daniel Finkel, "11 Days till Baghdad." *The Washington Post,* 25 February 2007, sec 1A, p. 1.

Colonel Kirby is then assigned to Vietnam, and Mr. Beckworth joins him to see what is happening 10,000 miles away. They go to a base camp (Camp 107) under construction near the Cambodian and Laotian borders. Eventually, the base is overrun by the NVA. Colonel Kirby and all the US forces retreat away from the camp. The scene ends with a "Puff the Magic Dragon" coming and killing every enemy soldier at the overrun base. The US forces then return, and Colonel Kirby pulls down the National Liberation Front (Viet Cong) flag that had been raised.

Mr. Beckman changes his view of the war based on the graphic and horrid descriptions of what the NVA and VC do to local villagers. He also befriends a young Vietnamese girl who is killed.

In a crucial scene, Colonel Kirby asks Mr. Beckman, "What are you going to say in that newspaper of yours?" Beckman replies, "If I say what I feel, I'll be out of a job."

John Wayne movies seem to portray a glorious enthusiasm for war. While he never served in the military, he probably influenced public opinion regarding going to war more than any other actor. *The Green Berets* is the only movie I know of made to show support for the war. In 1969, as a recently commissioned first lieutenant, I thought it portrayed reality as it was. We were fighting a noble cause to help a poor helpless country escape the jaws of godless communism. The "John Wayne Factor" convinced many Americans that our cause was noble and just. Unfortunately, I was a believer.

In Vietnam, I found that the picture portrayed by Wayne of war had no resemblance to the horrors of war. In the movie, wounded soldiers quietly lay on the ground. Those dying muttered poetic words giving the illusion that they were content with their plight. *The Green Berets* was nothing more than a propaganda epic. John Wayne's myth of noble war rings empty.

More recent films such as *Platoon* and *Saving Private Ryan* show the graphic rage of war. They offer the intense fear that overcomes the best soldier and, as best they can, the bloody savage wounds inflicted on men. But even these films fail to depict the battlefield's random, wanton, and graphic horror.

One afternoon in July of 2008, I was surfing channels on the TV. I came upon a health program on operations in a hospital emergency room. A boy of about 15 years was on the table in the ER being treated for a broken arm. The doctor asked him, "What do you want to do when you grow up?" He replied, "Join the army." She asked what he wanted to do in the army, and he replied, "I want to be in the infantry." She asked, "Why the infantry?" He said, "I like to shoot guns."

If he reaches his goal and serves his country during wartime, he may have asked for more than he had bargained for.

GIs in Vietnam who were in the infantry feared getting a "John Wayne" lieutenant. A John Wayne lieutenant would be "gung-ho" and possibly lead his men into needless combat. Unnecessary deaths would be the result.

I was not a "gung-ho" or "John Wayne" lieutenant. I was careful, organized, and systematic in what I did and asked my men to do. My concern for the brave men in my platoon was paramount. I have always been a planner and a thinker. That continued to be the case when I was in Vietnam. I believe it was a contributing factor to why no men in my platoon were killed while I was their platoon leader. In a tape to Sylvia, I was careful about everything I did. I said, "If I am careful, and I am, if I know what I am doing, and I do, I will be fine." I told her I had time to think when I was at the base camp and found that I missed her and my family more during those times. When I was in the jungle, I thought about what my men were doing, what they should be doing differently, what I had forgotten to do, and what I was missing in my planning. I told her, "If we were not the country that we are, we would not be helping the South Vietnamese; but then we would not be the country that we are."

Sometime it seems that war is necessary. Thomas Jefferson understood that when he said: "We will be soldiers, so our sons may be farmers, so their sons may be artists." In all cases it must be the last resort.

Sally Quinn was an Army brat. Her father fought in World War II and the Korean War. When she was 10, her father was in Korea. She fell ill from the trauma of her father being away and in danger. As a result, she ended up in a Tokyo Hospital. After nine months, she was transferred to a hospital in San Antonio. Her mother, brother, and sister accompanied her on the plane back to the States. She wrote about that plane ride: "The thing I remember most vividly is the soldiers screaming in pain and crying out for their mothers. My mother went up and down the aisles holding their hands, stroking their brows, giving them sips of water. My sister helped light their cigarettes. Many of them were amputees. Some had no stomachs; some had no faces. The soldiers in the litters above and below me both died, blood dripping from their wounds. Many other soldiers died while we were in the air. We had to stop in Hawaii overnight to refuel and to leave the bodies."[26]

In the spring and summer of 1969, I was a basic training unit training officer at Fort Benning, Georgia. One class was an ROTC class from a college. On one training exercise, we were being transported by bus to a training area. On the way, an ROTC recruit began talking to me about Vietnam. The fundamental justification for the war in Vietnam was that if South Vietnam fell to communism, all the countries in Southeast Asia would likewise fall like "dominos"; thus, Eisenhower developed the Domino Theory.

We know now that the theory was false. Southeast Asia did not fall to communism. In the 1980s, the Soviet Bloc in Eastern Europe fell like dominos. Communism could not maintain its iron grip on those countries; it had failed.

On October 31, 1969, when the VC soldier was scrambling to mount the warhead onto his RPG launcher, I rushed to fire my M-16 at him for fear of losing my life. I was not thinking of the United States flag, the National Anthem, or the Pledge of Allegiance. I did not visualize the Rocky Mountains in all their majesty, the mighty Grand Canyon in its grandeur, or purple waves of grain. I did not think of Duty, Honor, and Country. My mind and soul were not focused on

---

[26] Sally Quinn. "The Least Immoral Choice," *The Washington Post*, 9 January 2007, sec 1A, p. 15.

the rockets' red glare or bombs bursting in the air. My sole concentration was to, in some way, stay alive and live another day. Men do not die for their country. They die because their country sends them off to war.

During high school, I developed a keen interest in political matters. I was enamored by the anti-communist rhetoric of conservative politicians, writers, and speakers. I listened to Billy James Hargis's radio programs and was thrilled to hear him proclaim as he ended his broadcast with, "Jesus Christ is the hope of the world." Before that, he would rail against the evils of "godless communism." I ate it up. I would listen to all the conservative commentaries I could find on the radio. I attended several Young Americans for Freedom rallies with a local minister. I read the books by Barry Goldwater and loved his acceptance speech for the 1964 Republican nomination when he proclaimed, "...extremism in defense of liberty is no vice! And let me remind you also that moderation in the pursuit of justice is no virtue." I convinced my parents to put an AuH2O bumper sticker on our 1961 Ford station wagon. I was a patriotic American.

I was active in our Southern Baptist church youth group. I "hung out" with several guys in the group who shared my conservative agenda and views. One year the group sponsored a "Young Americans Want to Know" rally. We worked with our adult leaders to organize the event. We intended to spread spiritual and conservative themes at the rally. It was held on Friday, Saturday, and Sunday evenings. There was a small disappointing audience on Friday and Saturday evening but a good crowd on Sunday night. I thought I had done my part to increase my knowledge in such matters.

22

Waging Peace

"The arc of the moral universe is long, but it bends toward justice."

- Dr. Martin Luther King

I participated in my first demonstration on a Sunday evening in March 2003. It was a week before the United States invaded Iraq. The event was called a "candlelight vigil" and took place at many locations worldwide at 6:00 p.m. local time. The one in Washington, DC, was at the Lincoln Memorial base with the reflecting pool as a backdrop. Peter, Paul, and Mary performed their classic peace songs.

In 1969, Sylvia and her family attended a demonstration supporting the soldiers in Vietnam on the Mall of Washington, DC. She and her sister, Judy, were minding their business when they were suddenly in the middle of a brick-throwing bunch of troublemakers. She will never forget that as her only experience in a demonstration. So, she was reluctant for me to go, fearing there might be "trouble" at such an event.

My experience in 2003 was quite different. It was quiet, peaceful, reflective, and inspiring. Upon returning from Vietnam, I promised myself I would "do my part" to promote peace on this planet and protest wars that I considered unnecessary and unjust. I thought the Iraq War to be both. I felt good and fulfilled by participating in the vigil.

I retired in June 2005. Retirement has given me the time to write this book along with *Mr. NewHeart - From Heart Attack to Transplant and Beyond,* which is my 1991 heart transplant story. It has also allowed me to participate in events that were not possible while working.

One such event was the September 9 to 11, 2005, display of "Eyes Wide Open" in Baltimore on the campus of Johns Hopkins University. The American Friends Service Committee (www.afsc.org/eyes) sponsored it, and its purpose was to memorialize the lives lost in the Iraq War. The exhibit included a pair of boots symbolizing each US military casualty. There was a field of shoes and a wall of remembrance memorializing the Iraqi deaths. I was one of 150 volunteers helping at the Baltimore exhibit. I handed out flyers about the display to passersby on campus.

When the exhibit began in January 2004, 504 pairs of boots symbolized US soldiers' lost lives in Iraq. Each week, at each stop in a new city, more pairs of boots were added to represent the newly fallen. Over 3,000 pairs of boots were displayed in 2006, and the total deaths reached over 4,400 at the war's end.

In May 2006, the AFSC sponsored another Eyes Wide Open exhibit on the Mall in Washington, DC. It was labeled "Silence of the Dead, Voices of the Living." I visited the display one afternoon. It was a sad day for me.

> "Eisenhower repeatedly referred to the fact that the strength of a nation lies ultimately not in arms but in its ability to provide decently for its people. In a speech titled 'The Chance for Peace,' he listed all the schools and hospitals that the US could build for the cost of one bomber, and declared 'This is not a way of life at all, in any true sense. Under a cloud of threatening war, it is humanity hanging from a cross of iron.'"[27]

The United States Institute of Peace is located in Washington, DC. "...is a national, nonpartisan, independent

---

[27] John Hulsman and Anatol Lieven. "The neocons got us into Iraq, but Ike should take if from here," *The Free Lance-Star,* 12 January 2007, sec. 1A, p. 9.

institute, founded by Congress and dedicated to the proposition that a world without violent conflict is possible, practical and essential for U.S. and global security. In conflict zones abroad, the Institute works with local partners to prevent, mitigate, and resolve violent conflict. To reduce future crises and the need for costly interventions, USIP works with governments and civil societies to build local capacities to manage conflict peacefully. The Institute pursues its mission by linking research, policy, training, analysis and direct action to support those who are working to build a more peaceful, inclusive world."[28] I attended several sessions there that were open to the public.

Today, as always, war is a right-to-life issue. The act of going to war is guided by the "just-war theory," involving justifying going to war in the first place. It also addresses the methods of conducting a war once it has been deemed just. The significant elements of the just-war theory are:

- That war is the only means whereby a nation can protect itself.
- That all alternatives to war have been exhausted.
- That the good achieved outweighs the evil that is done.
- That there be an avoidance of civilian casualties.

While examining the just-war theory, we must also consider what the Bible tells us about pursuing peace. Jesus said, "You have heard that it was said, 'Love your neighbor and hate your enemy.' But I tell you: Love your enemies and pray for those who persecute you." (Matthew 5:43-44) The Prophet described the coming Messiah as the "prince of peace." (Isaiah 9:6) A great company of heavenly hosts proclaimed, "Glory to God in the highest, and on earth peace to men on whom his favor rests." (Luke 2:14) When Jesus entered Jerusalem, he proclaimed, "If you, even you, had only known on this day what would bring you peace—but now it is hidden from your eyes." (Luke 19:42) Paul declared that there is a gospel of peace, "...and with your feet fitted with the readiness that comes from the gospel of peace," (Ephesians 3:19). Righteousness or justice will bring peace, "The fruit of righteousness will be peace; the effect of

---

[28] https://www.usip.org/about

righteousness will be quietness and confidence forever." (Isaiah, 32:17). "Love and faithfulness meet together; righteousness and peace kiss each other." (Psalm 34:14) We are to reject our natural sinful instincts and strive to be Christ-like.

But I tell you who hear me: Love your enemies, do good to those who hate you, bless those who curse you, pray for those who mistreat you. If someone strikes you on one cheek, turn to him on the other. If someone takes your cloak, do not stop him from taking your tunic. Give to everyone who asks you, and if anyone takes what belongs to you, do not demand it back. Do to others as you would have them do to you." (Luke 6:27)

Paul admonishes us not to "...take revenge, my friends, but leave room for God's wrath, for it is written: 'It is mine to avenge; I will repay,' says the Lord. On the contrary. "If your enemy is hungry, feed him; if he is thirsty, give him something to drink." (Romans 12:19). We are to pray "...your kingdom come; your will be done on earth as it is in heaven." (Matthew 6:10) We are to strive for a Christ-like environment on earth, as it will be in heaven.

Peacemakers must be proactive. Peace will not just "happen." Jimmy Carter has gained far more respect for his peacemaking work out of office than he ever did as president, but wouldn't it be even better if heads of state were committed to peacemaking while they had the political power? However, what Carter and others have shown is the powerful potential to resolve terrible conflicts. Most of the world's conflicts are actually resolved in peaceful ways. Domestic disputes over a host of policy issues are resolved daily without recourse to violence. Peacemaking is simply the attempt to expand the number of conflicts resolved with nonviolent means.

Professor Glen Stassen of Pasadena's Fuller Theological Seminary published *Just Peacemaking: Ten Practices for Abolishing War*. The 10 steps outline how to approach the task of peacemaking in our world. Jim Wallis's book, *Faith Works*, presents those steps on pages 229-232. I challenge the reader to obtain that book, study the steps, and urge our leaders to apply them to their decision-making. Better yet, get and read Stassen's book.

Christians know that "there is more to the story" of waging peace. We realize and understand that true peace will only come as a gift of God. Many people in recent years are dwelling on the "end times." The *Left Behind* series of books has heightened Christians' and nonbelievers' interest in the subject. While we look to the future of Christ, reigning for 1,000 years in an environment of world peace, we must remember that we live in the here and now. We should pursue peaceful solutions in our own lives and the activities and actions of nations. The Bible teaches this to us.

Billy Graham puts it this way: "When God decries it, Satan (Lucifer) will be removed from the world of disorder so God can establish righteousness everywhere and a true theocracy. Not until that event takes place will the human race know perfect **peace** on earth." (Emphasis added.)[29]

General Wesley K. Clark (US Army) was the former supreme commander of NATO. He was the senior commander in 1999 when the alliance went to war to stop Slobodan Milosevic from repressing the ethnic Albanian population in Kosovo, and he was a candidate for President in 2004. In 2007, he lamented, "The best war is the one that doesn't have to be fought, and the best military is capable and versatile enough to deter the next war in the first place."[30] I pray that our leaders will heed such wisdom.

In December 2005, a friend gave me a Christmas subscription to *The Economist* magazine. You probably think the magazine is about nothing but the "dismal science." However, nothing could be further from the truth. It is a magazine about what is happening in countries around our planet. True, it has an economic and business leaning, but it addresses many other topics.

One thing became abundantly clear after the first three or four issues. My dear United States of America is only ONE of many countries on terra firma. Of course, I knew that from

---

[29] Billy Graham, *Angels: God's Secret Agents* (Doubleday & Company, 1975), 133.
[30] General Wesley Clark (Ret.), "The Next War", *The Washington Post*, 16 September 2007, sec. B, p. 1.

Geography class in the 10th grade. Nevertheless, I saw all those articles about Sweden, Norway, China, Argentina, Burma, etc. People living in all of the world's countries likely tend to think only of their own country. Most people have never seen, much less ever, read even one article in *The Economist* magazine (circulation is over 1.6 million - nearly eight billion people on our planet). The almost two million people who read the magazine see the world from a different and much broader perspective. I think it is unfortunate that not everyone on earth can see the collective "us." If we all did, we would have better respect and understanding of ourselves and everyone else.

Executions of government officials are common, so many don't take their jobs out of fear. Regardless of how just war may meet all of the criteria of a "just war," the execution of warfare inevitably, usually sooner than later, gravitates to the dark side - - and becomes evil. It's a situation replicated across the southern provinces dominated by the Taliban. The campaign mirrored Viet Cong tactics in the early years of the Vietnam War when government officials were assassinated — more than 400 in 1957 alone — to undermine the South Vietnamese government at the local level. In turn, more than 26,000 Viet Cong members were assassinated between 1968 and 1972 under a secret US operation known as the Phoenix Program.[31]

Peace does not come easily or automatically. It must be waged. Diplomacy must be exhausted before we take up arms.

The 52 Iranian hostages were released from captivity on January 20, 1981, when Ronald Reagan was sworn in as president. On Tuesday, January 27, they were bused through Washington, DC in a patriotic parade. Thousands of screaming people attended the event. Excessive patriotism was on display.

A conservative coworker and friend took time off to go to the parade. When he returned, he popped open my office door with a huge smile on his face and proclaimed "I AM READY TO GO TO WAR." I was stunned! I worked for the

---

[31] http://www.msnbc.msn.com/id/38476852/ns/world_news-south_and_central_asia/ - Accessed August 2, 2010

General Services Administration of the federal government in Washington.

He did not serve in the military but was ready to send 19-year-olds to war. He had no idea what war was like. None! This type of militaristic thinking impedes Waging Peace.

23

The Night

"Not Waving but Drowning"
- poem by Stevie Smith

I returned home from Vietnam on August 15, 1970; I thought the war was over for my family and me. I realized that instead of being over, it had just begun in many ways. Upon returning home, I started a journey common to every Vietnam veteran. Whether it was day or night in America, we started our difficult and long journey "Into the Night" before we could climb "Out of the Night." In some ways, for many, the Vietnam War was a journey into spiritual darkness. It became the blackest night of the soul. Some succumbed to suicide. Others were condemned to a lifetime of depression and sadness. Many others were able to go on with their lives and attain their life goals.

Depression took a terrible toll on my family and me. In a session with my counselor Elaine. I told her, "At some level, the Vietnam War almost ruined my life." That was because of the results of the depression that it brought upon me.

I have seen the face of war. It is a terrible ordeal. It never smiles. It only cries in anguish, terror, and pain. It is the face of widows and fatherless children. That face is always the same, whether in world wars, Korea, Vietnam, Iraq, or Afghanistan. In Vietnam, GIs learned that it was impossible to kill without emotional engagement.

In 1980 the Vietnam Veterans of America (VVA) organization was formed by veterans of that war. It was created because Vietnam veterans, for the most part, were rejected when we came home. There were no parades, accolades, parties, or recognition. All too often, veterans of WWII and Korea thought we were not veterans of a "real" war. Some considered us to be "crybabies" and weak. We were sometimes not allowed to join organizations such as the Veterans of Foreign Wars or the American Legion. For that reason, the VVA slogan is, "Never again will one generation of veterans abandon another."

Sticker on our 1998 Chevrolet Lumina

Not long after my return my oldest brother, Paul, was visiting us. He told me that while I was not nearby, he asked Sylvia how I was doing. He said she hesitated and only said, "He has changed." Sylvia has told me that she has commented to some of her lady friends at church that "the person who went to Vietnam (her husband) is not the same person who came back." Sylvia has told me that if I were like the person I had become after Vietnam, she probably would not have married me when we met.

Because of these comments, I titled this book *Casualties of War*. The casualties extend far beyond those killed or physically wounded and their families. It includes the many thousands of soldiers who are plagued by PTSD, Agent Orange, and depression. It is an ailment that affects everyone around them.

After the war, I found that hardly anyone wanted to know anything about my experience. That was fine because I did not want to talk about it. Years later, my brother, Paul, told me I would not say anything about it. He would ask questions that I would never answer. Americans often wanted to forget about the war and think of it as never happening. But it did happen. That rejection was a significant factor in my coming emotional storm.

Upon returning home, I returned to working at Arthur Andersen & Co. as a junior auditor. When I started there in June 1967, I was one of about 25 new junior auditors after college graduation. Only two or three were left when I returned in February 1971. It was typical for large auditing firms to have a significant turnover of their new junior auditors. Of those remaining, they were three years ahead of me in experience and salary.

Unlike when I first began working at Arthur Andersen, I had more difficulty concentrating and understanding the work. One morning in April, my senior supervisory auditor told me to report to David Ellis, the Office Manager, the following day. Ellis said I was not working out with the firm and recommended that I look for a position elsewhere. Since I was a veteran and had entered the Army after working at Arthur Andersen, they were required to keep me for one year if that was what I wanted. I told him I did not want to do that and would look for another job. Being dismissed from my first accounting job was difficult, humiliating, and embarrassing.

I remained on the payroll during the 12 weeks I looked for a new position. I did not go to the office because Mr. Ellis said, "your full-time job is to find another one."

My experience of being dismissed convinced me that I did not ever want to go through such an ordeal again. Since we lived near Washington, DC, I decided to find a position with the federal government where job security was more likely. I received a job offer at Woodward & Lothrop department store as an internal audit manager at $11,000 a year. My starting salary at GSA would be $10,800, but I needed the government position's security.

I began working in the Office of Finance of the General Services Administration in early August. While there, I earned a CPA certificate in Maryland, became a supervisor, and eventually retired in 2005 after 37 years of federal service, including three years in the Army.

Most male employees in my age bracket at GSA had not served in the military. They were at grades GS-11 or GS-12 (at salaries of $12,500 or $15,000, respectively), while I started at GS-9 ($10,800). I knew well the salary gap that serving my country had cost us. It amounted to a lot of money. During slow work periods, I would calculate how much the gap was at that time and the impact over 20 years. Such thinking, I expect, fueled my cynicism over the years.

On April 2, 1982, Argentina invaded the British colony on the Falkland Islands 400 miles from Argentine soil. It was nearly 7,500 miles from the British mainland. The population at the time was less than 2,000 people and 400,000 sheep. On the 5th of April, a British task force set out on the British 7,500-mile journey to liberate the islands. That effort began the most extensive naval action since the Second World War, and nearly 900 men lost their lives.

I read an article about the war in a newspaper. It included an interview with a young British Marine Lieutenant. He commented that war was not what he expected. He said it was more terrible than anything he had ever imagined. Much of the war was fought at night, which would have made battles all the more terrifying, especially to a lieutenant responsible for 30 men.

As I read the article, I found myself muttering aloud. "Now you know what it is like, and you will never forget it. You may try, but you will likely fail."

One day after I returned home, Sylvia and I went to a park for a picnic. There were many trees in the area, just like the jungles of Vietnam. I was continually alert for noises like bristling bushes or squirrels running about. I had left Vietnam, but it had not left me. I was a Casualty of War.

In 1991 I was the recipient of a heart transplant. I am receiving compensation from the Veterans Administration for heart disease caused by exposure to Agent Orange in Vietnam's jungles. A side effect was kidney failure, for which I am also receiving compensation. I also filed a claim for PTSD in 2012, which was also approved.

In 2007 my book, *Mr. NewHeart – From Heart Attack to Transplant and Beyond,* was published. It tells the story of my transplant. On page 57, I wrote this regarding the returning trauma of the war:

> As I have mentioned, I am a Vietnam veteran. I served as an infantry platoon leader with the First Infantry Division in 1969 and 1970. I experienced the pain of returning to a country where many were disillusioned with the war and its veterans. Over the years, I had "worked through" that pain and come to some resolution within my being and soul. I was distressed to realize that these mental, emotional, and spiritual demons from my Vietnam experience had returned as I tried to deal with my heart disease and transplant.

The transplant surgery took place on Easter Sunday, March 31, 1991. Over a 20-month period, I was hospitalized for over eight months. I was discharged from the George Washington University hospital in Washington, D.C. on May 6 and returned to work at GSA in January, 1992.

Not long after returning to work, I realized something was wrong. I found that there was a change in me after the transplant. It was something that had materialized in addition to the ordeal of the heart attack, surgery, and recovery.

I lacked the confidence level I possessed before the heart transplant. I did not feel comfortable doing things that were routine before my transplant. I feared getting an assignment that I thought I could not handle. That feeling was new to me; I had never had hesitation about my projects. The merger of the two traumas (combat and heart disease) seemed to have released hidden emotional and psychological issues that negatively impacted my performance. Once again, I had become a Casualty of War.

It came to the point that I talked to my supervisor about my issues with some assignments. He said that he would see that I did not receive such assignments. Making such a presentation to one's boss pretty much eliminates any thoughts of a promotion.

That supervisor moved on to other assignments in about a year as my feelings continued. Over the next 10 years, I was in various situations that I considered beyond my capabilities. I could not remember the rules and regulations for areas I was responsible for (travel and accounts receivable policy) and that were required to do my job. I would read them and could not recall them the next day.

When we returned home from Vietnam, we were expected to become law-abiding distinguished citizens of our country. Hours earlier, we had left a country where death, dismemberment, and destruction were the expected norm. There was no counseling or instruction on becoming one of millions of citizens going about their daily activities in their respective communities.

No one warned us that there would be flashbacks, nightmares, and post-traumatic stress to greet us with our return to the "world." No one had told us of the impending diseases caused by exposure to Agent Orange. Few understood where we had been, what we had done, the things we had seen, touched, and smelled. Few understood why we were sent to "Nam" in the first place. Even fewer wanted to know. Unless we had an understanding family, we were on our own. Some did not make it. There have been an estimated 9.000 suicides by Vietnam veterans.

When our son Mike was born in 1972, I became fearful that in 20 years, he might be fighting in another war. One day I purchased the book *War Through the Ages* by Lynn Montross. It is a 1,088-page description of battles from 490 B.C up to but not including Vietnam. Sylvia asked me why

I bought it. I told her that if I could do anything to prevent Mike from having to go to war, I would. The book might help me in attaining that goal.

Several years ago, I saw a play entitled *An Iliad*. It is a captivating monologue of the Trojan War. It tells the story of the war and highlights the current fact of humanity's attraction to violence. It leads the viewer to wonder "What, if anything, had changed since the Trojan War."

At one point in the play, the storyteller lists the wars' names. It took several minutes and was a powerful and moving presentation. It made me think that "war is an evil venture."

Finally, in August 2011, I began counseling with Elaine (not her real name), a Christian counselor. It was something I should have done a couple of decades earlier. Sylvia and I were hesitant about going, not knowing whether it would help or make things worse. I began my first session with Elaine by summarizing my Vietnam and heart disease experiences. After I finished, Elaine said: "Dave, what you are saying is that things that you thought should be the standard, the way things should be, were completely upended and shattered?" I replied, "That's exactly what happened to me." At that point, I was nearly sure that counseling would help. I had confidence in her.

I continue to see Elaine about every six weeks. I went to her because of depression but found it was PTSD also. Counseling was tremendously helpful. After about a month, the depression was mainly GONE.

Research has shown that traumatic events result in changes in the brain. Such differences make it all the more difficult to recover. Recovery takes a tremendous amount of effort and takes a long time. We know that PTSD is not the result of a person's failures. "We now know that their (PTSD) behavior are not the result of moral failings or signs of lack of willpower or bad character – they are caused by changes in the brain."[32]

---

[32] Bessel Van Der Kolk, M.D. *The Body Keeps the Score – Brain, Mind, and Body in the Healing of Trauma* (Penguin Books, 2014), 3.

Elaine pointed out that I had experienced double traumas (combat and heart disease/transplant) which made my case all the more complicated. She noted that the second one would often bring back the first in a fury when someone has two traumas. That is what happened to me. While in the hospital for heart ailments, I found myself dwelling on the war along with the heart. After a month or so of counseling, the frequent bouts of depression diminished significantly.

A significant issue for me in counseling was the army recruiters giving me misinformation about how to become a lieutenant in the Army Finance Corps. I had a session in April, 2013 with my counselor where we addressed that matter. At one point, I clenched my fists, leaned forward, and exclaimed that "they had no right to do that to me."

By this time, I had been going to counseling for eight months. Elaine could see that I was in great distress. She said, "Dave, you're stuck, and I want to try something different." She suggested I agree to use Eye Movement Desensitization and Reprocessing (EMDR). It was developed in 1989 by psychologist Francine Shapiro. It is commonly used to treat PTSD. I agreed to give it a try and found that it was beneficial.

I told Elaine that I had become cynical and critical about nearly everything and that I was not like that before going to Vietnam. I also told her that the counseling helped me feel able to begin to live again.

Sylvia has said that two events brought the war back to the front burner:

1. Heart disease
2. The 2003 invasion of Iraq

After Vietnam, I found that I would become irritated or angry very quickly. I was quick to judge, cynical about everything, and intolerant. It was decades before I realized why. Even with counseling it continues today. I am a Casualty of War.

Karl Marlentes was a marine infantry lieutenant in Vietnam. He was featured in *The Vietnam War* documentary by Ken Burns. In it, he describes an event that took place after returning home. He was in his car, and the driver behind him honked his horn. The next thing he knew, he was on the hood of that car, pounding on the window and yelling at the driver. He had no idea that his reaction was a result of the war. I have had multiple experiences similar to Marlentes but without violence.

I experienced things that I now realize were from PTSD. I did not understand why I became so angry over so little at the time. When I was in a car alone, I would often scream, yell and swear at anything and everything – cars, drivers, the wind, a tree, the sky, anything. I had a very supportive wife and family but could not fully share what I had been through. Still today, a sudden noise will startle me and cause me to come to the alert stage. It is not just loud noises. Any sudden noise, regardless of the volume, will initiate the reaction. It happens when Sylvia is washing the dishes, and I am beside her drying them. A pot tapping against the side of the sink will cause an immediate response.

Through the years, the impact of the war on me continued in the form of becoming angry quickly, using strong language (usually in private), being cynical about anything and everything. I was also angry about our unusually high number and intensity of life's difficulties.

This condition caused me to be less understanding or supportive of Sylvia than I needed to be. She could sense when I was having a bad time. Those times came without warning, and I could not explain it to myself or her. It seemed that I had changed dramatically and drastically from the 25-year-old who was sent to Vietnam.

Sometime after the transplant, I began having bouts of being very tired, accompanied by headaches. Doctors have never determined the cause, and it continues to the present day although less frequently. These occurrences would last anywhere from a day to a couple of weeks. The only relief was taking Tylenol and getting extra rest and sleep.

When Sylvia saw that I was struggling, she often asked: "Is it mental, physical, or both?" Too often it would be mental. I have often wondered how many wives, with any regularity, ask their husbands that question. I expect the answer is not many.

Depression would descend over me at any time. There would be no warning, which would command our lives for that time. I would go to bed and cry for five or 10 minutes without knowing why. Once in an email, my brother Paul asked why I was depressed. I replied that I did not know. I talked about it very little because I could not see the problem, so how could anyone else?

I remember the details of one episode. It was on my birthday, and we were in Fredericksburg, VA. I had been having mental issues that day and maybe a few days before. We celebrated by having lunch at Brock's restaurant. Sylvia's sister owned a store in the Old Towne section of the city. After lunch, we went there to visit. We parked on the street near the store. I told Sylvia to go in and I would be in soon. While in the car alone, I cried with huge uncontrollable gasps for air as the depression demons escaped from my body. It lasted nearly 10 minutes.

After episodes like that, I felt so much better. Feeling better could last a month or two or more. Then again, it might be only two weeks, one week, or a couple of days when the demons were back, and the cycle repeated. I believe the root cause of this condition was the war and the heart transplant, both of which were life-threatening traumatic events.

Each year an air show was performed at the Andrews Air Base near our home. One year Sylvia and I went to it. They had scores of military aircraft on display including bombers. Walking under one of them, I pointed out to Sylvia where the bombs were stored. The bomb doors were open.

I began to feel uneasy and nervous. At one point, in the distance, the Army was executing a combat air assault to the area with choppers bringing in infantry troops onto the ground. That was it. I told Sylvia that I had to leave, and we did.

At GSA, I relied on my staff for too many things because I could not handle them. I would become very flustered, tense, and confused whenever I needed to handle multiple tasks simultaneously. A significant problem was conducting a meeting or participating in one that involved what I considered complex matters. My supervisor handled things that I should have mastered.

Another example of my limits was when I arranged a retirement luncheon for two employees. Everyone in the branch, plus my supervisor, went to a Friday's restaurant near the office. At the end of the meal, the server brought the bill and gave a pitch to join their Friday's club.

For most people, this would have been a nothing event. For me, it was just the opposite. I had to calculate what each of those at the table owed me (we paid for the two retirees) along with the tip. At the same time, that server presented me with another complication – the offer to join their members club.

I could not handle the multiple tasks of determining what each person owed and analyzing the server's offer. It was utterly overwhelming to me. So, I said "No" to the server abruptly so that she would not pursue the matter any further. My supervisor was sitting beside me and said something to the effect of, "That was a brush-off!" I did not reply. I knew I could not handle the third issue.

It came to a climax in the spring of 2005 with a new supervisor. She assumed I could do things that my previous supervisor had done himself (stuff I should have been able to handle). Within four months, I could see that it was getting out of hand. It got to the point that I hated going to work. I dreaded every day, every hour. All too often, I would go into the men's room, look to see that it was empty, go into a stall, and cry because I did not know how to handle things. My world had collapsed again. So, at the end of April 2005, I told Sylvia I needed to get out. I needed to retire to escape the torment. I did retire on June 3.

A second event that brought back Vietnam memories was the 2003 invasion of Iraq. It was another war that I considered unnecessary and a mistake. The memories of my combat experiences resurfaced.

Sylvia tells me that I changed after the heart transplant, and Vietnam was back on the front burner– my feelings of betrayal came back.

Jonathan Shay (Ph.D., MD) is the author of *Achilles in Vietnam – Combat Trauma and the Undoing of Character.* In an April 2010 interview with PBS, he describes Moral Injury to soldiers as: *"Betrayal of what is right by someone who holds legitimate authority in a high stakes situation."*

This happened to me due to events before, during, and after my service in Vietnam. I have told family and friends that "for me, the Vietnam War changed everything." The causes of that change have three elements:

- How I became an infantry lieutenant.
- After the war, I realized that I believed that the war was a mistake and should not have happened.
- How we were treated (mistreated) upon our return home.

First, I became an infantry lieutenant because of misstatements by multiple U.S. Army recruiters. But, in my mind, it went much further. The misstatements came from my government, my country. Years after returning from Vietnam, I learned that being in the infantry was a rare occupation in the military. No more than one in 10 troops are front-line infantry in any significant military operation.

Second, after the war, I realized that the domino theory (created by Eisenhower and perpetrated by Kennedy, Johnson, and Nixon) was false. It was the basic foundation used for going to war. The war ended via Nixon's Vietnamization (i.e., let's get the hell out of there) program. The conflict in Vietnam was not a significant player in communist expansion; it was an internal revolution, and therefore we should not have been there.

I had been sent to a war that should not have happened. I was sent to a war our leaders (JFK, LBJ, and Nixon) knew was not winnable. It was a war that much of the country despised. My country had misled me.

Third, the country that sent us to war and rejected us upon our return home. All three of these issues betrayed what is right by those in authority and a high-stake situation. They all resulted in my Moral Injury.

I experienced depression during the two years between the heart attack and heart transplant in 1991. However, the depression returned in 1994. I was prescribed anti-depressant medication.

The betrayals prompted me to tell my counselor on December 19, 2011: "At some level, the Vietnam War ruined my life" I said that because of the resulting significant impact of depression on my family and me over several decades. I have continued taking prescribed antidepressants since 1994.

I have problems remembering events that recently occurred and have developed a cynical attitude and suspiciousness toward people and organizations. Loud and unexpected noises, including voices, startled me and made me feel disoriented. Other veterans have told me that they have the same issue. I find that my mood varies and changes from hour to hour and day to day. I have significant difficulty in attempting to accomplish multiple tasks simultaneously. Such attempts are usually not successful.

The war negatively impacted millions of Americans. Dunbar's number is the limit to the number of people with whom one can maintain ongoing social relationships. It was developed by Robin Dunbar, a British anthropologist, in the 1990s. He determined that people can have about 150 stable relationships. He said it was "the number of people you would not feel embarrassed about joining uninvited for a drink if you happened to bump into them in a bar." [33]

The number of GIs killed in the war was 58,220, and 153,000 were wounded. Using Dunbar's number, the losses negatively impacted 8,733,000 family members' and friends' lives. The number affected grows to 22,950,000 when factoring in the number who were wounded. The Vietnam War left us with millions of Casualties of War.

---

[33] https://en.wikipedia.org/wiki/Dunbar%27s_number

24

Out of the Night

"The world breaks everyone and afterward many are strong at the broken places."
- Ernest Hemmingway

A healing event was when I participated in an Oral History when Joe Galloway interviewed me. He has conducted over 800 interviews with Vietnam veterans. He is doing a marvelous job helping vets come Out of the Night.

When the 2003 invasion of Iraq began in March, it brought to mind the Vietnam War. A First Infantry Division Monument was only a 10-minute walk from my office. One day during lunch, I decided to visit it. The memorial is behind the Old Executive Office building near the White House. During the growing season, a big number one is created by hundreds of red roses. It was a moving sight.

The memorial includes a tall Victory Statue at the apex. On the sides of the statue are large plaques with First Infantry Division men killed in combat in WWI, WWII, Korea, and Vietnam. I spent most of my time in front of the Vietnam War plaque. Seeing the names of soldiers I knew right in front of me was a chilling sight.

On March 12, 1989, I suffered a major heart attack. It was a complete surprise because I had no risk factors associated with heart disease. Over the coming months, my condition deteriorated to the point that I received a heart transplant in March 1991. During these two years, memories of the trauma of Vietnam came to the surface. I later learned that a second traumatic, life-threatening event would bring back a previous one. Years later, I realized that my heart disease was caused by exposure to Agent Orange in Vietnam.

During the two years, I was hospitalized for over eight months. I received counseling from psychiatrists on the hospital staff. I found that I was talking about the war as much as my immediate heart condition. It was a terrible combination! I was dealing with two traumatic events as if they were happening right then.

In November 1982, the Vietnam Veterans Memorial was dedicated. Sylvia, myself, and Mike attended the dedication. It was a difficult, moving, and healing day. The memorial is only a 10-minute walk from my office at GSA. While it was being constructed, I would go to the site to see the progress.

On March 18, 2003, the United States began an Iraq invasion to neutralize weapons of mass destruction that were believed to be present. Most Americans supported the invasion.

Any knowledgeable American knows that the soldiers that served in Iraq from 2003 to 2011 received uncounted accolades from the American people. Television news reports show soldiers debarking from a plane, bringing them back from their tour in Iraq. Passengers in the airport spontaneously stand as they enter the room and applaud their sacrifices and service as they march by.

One day in 2004, while I was in our local grocery store, I noticed an Army captain, with a woman I assumed was his wife. He was dressed in desert fatigues. I approached them and asked if he had just returned from Iraq. He replied, "Yes." I thanked him for answering his country's call. I told him I was an Infantry Army Officer in Vietnam and that no one ever stopped me on the street to thank me for anything. He replied, "I think that is part of the reason the public gives us such strong support - because you guys did not get any."

On November 20, 2006, my 91-year-old mother-in-law fell and broke her arm. Sylvia spent several months staying with her in Fredericksburg, Virginia, while she healed and recovered. I would alternate my time between Fredericksburg and our home in Maryland.

On January 6, 2007, I was in Fredericksburg. It was my custom to go to McDonald's in the early morning for coffee. That morning, I noticed about half a dozen Army soldiers dressed in desert fatigues when I entered the restaurant. I had never seen soldiers there in the past. I stopped at a table where two were sitting and asked them what was happening in town. One replied that there was a dinner that night for them and that the next day they were headed for Fort Dix, New Jersey, for two months of training and then would be deployed to southern Iraq for 18 months. I talked to them for a few minutes and told them I was an infantry lieutenant in Vietnam and had gone to basic training at Fort Dix. I wished them good luck and turned to order my coffee. As I left the table, my lips began to quiver, and my eyes became watery. I had to concentrate on controlling it as I ordered the coffee. I was troubled with their having to go to Iraq, knowing that some may lose an eye, a leg, an arm, all three, or their life.

When I returned to my mother-in-law's apartment, I saw an article in the Fredericksburg paper about the soldiers. The report identified them as nearly 200 members of the Virginia National Guard from Fredericksburg and Leesburg, Virginia. They would leave from the Fredericksburg Armory the following morning at 9:30 a.m. and proceed down Caroline Street for a public sendoff. I decided that I wanted to participate in that sendoff.

I arrived at Caroline Street at about 9:15 a.m. and waited for the caravan of soldiers. It was a chilly but sunny January morning. The street was dotted with spectators waiting for the event to begin. One woman held a sign that read, "Thank You, God Bless You." Many had flags. Each street lamp had a flag attached to its top. A fire truck with a long ladder had parked on a side street facing Caroline Street. The extension ladder protruded over the center of the street, making an inverted "V." Hanging from the ladder was a large American flag under which the soldiers would ride.

I heard a siren at 9:50 a.m. I looked to my left and saw the first of four coach buses turning from Lafayette Boulevard onto Caroline Street, led by a police car with lights flashing. As the buses rolled by, the small crowd cheered and waved. The soldiers were waving back. They passed in 30 seconds and continued down Caroline Street, making a left turn at the end. They were beginning their journey to Iraq. As the buses disappeared, I wondered how many of them would return in 18 months alive and healthy.

As these soldiers were preparing to deploy to Iraq, 150 National Guardsmen were cheered in Richmond, Virginia, 50 miles south of Fredericksburg. They were to soldiers of the 654th Military Police Company just returning from a year in Iraq. They provided security for high-level Iraqi government officials and trained Iraqi police forces in Baghdad. Sgt. Michael Putnam, 48, of Williamsburg, expressed the crowd's feelings: "We are so blessed to live in the land of liberty."[34]

Reunions of Bravo Company were helpful in recovering from the war. The first one I attended was in 2006 in Nashville, Tennessee. Jerry Wilson organized it. There was good attendance. I also attended the next one in 2008. Several guys that were in my platoon were also there. It was really great to see them and talk about old times in Vietnam.

Mike platoon at 2008 reunion

---

[34] Associated Press. "Virginia Guard unit returns from Iraq," *The Free Lance-Star,* 8 January 2007.

In 2014 there was a reunion of my company in the Washington, D.C. area near our home. Sixteen attended. It was great to see all of them and talk about our experiences.

One evening a bus tour was scheduled of the D.C. sites. One of the destinations was the Lincoln Memorial. We stopped there and looked around. At one point I was standing on extensive steps up to the statue when two teen agers approached me. I though they would be selling something. Instead, they said "Welcome Home." It nearly brought tears to my eyes.

Bravo Company reunion in 2014
In front of the statue to the Vietnam Veterans Memorial statue

In 2014 I attended a reunion of army guys in Pigeon Forge, Tennessee. It was sponsored by the battalion instead of just Bravo Company. It was a good experience.

L to R, Marshall Copeland, Bob Gadd, Jim Fletcher, Dave Hollar, who were in my platoon

2014 reunion

During the weekend of June 18-19, 2016, Maryland Public Television sponsored a time for Vietnam veterans to gather together to focus on a tribute for their service. It was called "LZ Maryland." Unfortunately, I was pretty ill that weekend and unable to attend. Still, seeing the station sponsor such an event was a great encouragement.

In October 2015, the Southern High School of Anne Arundel County, Maryland, sponsored a "Maryland Veterans: A Journey through Vietnam" event. It was very lovely and appreciated. They also arranged for their students to conduct oral histories of Vietnam vets. I participated and appreciated their efforts.

In May 2023 The United State Vietnam War Commemoration organization sponsored a three-day event in Washington, D.C. to honor, recognize, and thank Vietnam Veterans and their families for their service and sacrifice. It featured static helicopter displays and more than 40 exhibit tents featuring museum displays. It was a very important occasion that helped to improve the images of Vietnam Veterans.

In Philippians 4:6-7, Paul tells us to: "Be anxious for nothing, but in everything by prayer and supplication, with thanksgiving, let your requests be made known to God; and the peace of God, which surpasses all understanding, will guard your hearts and minds through Christ Jesus." This is not an easy goal for a victim who experienced combat. Climbing Out of the Night has been a full-time effort for me. It is the work of a lifetime.

My journey Out of the Night significantly accelerated when I began counseling in August 2011. It has been a long, arduous effort and journey. *Shattered Assumptions: Towards a New Psychology of Trauma* by Ronnie Janoff-Bulman was the first book that Elaine recommended to me. It addresses the concept of Schemas. They are how a person sees the world as it is supposed to be, not necessarily as it is. During my first session, I described my issues in detail. She responded like this: "You mean, Dave, that the things you thought were firm and solid, that was the way everything should be, was SHATTERED." I replied that it was exactly what had happened to me. My fundamental assumptions about my bedrock of concepts about life were shredded. I thought America always wore a white hat regarding the Vietnam War. I felt that the Army and my government would never mislead me. Both did. I did all the right things regarding the heart transplant--exercising and eating a healthy diet--but I still succumbed to life-threatening heart disease. Later I learned that the cause was exposure to Agent Orange in Vietnam. So, the war followed me home years later.

In 2020 I needed to see a vascular surgeon, regarding blood circulation in my right leg. He asked me about my medical history. After describing my litany of medical ailments, he asked, "How did you come to get all these conditions at such a young age?"

I replied that I was exposed to Agent Orange in Vietnam. He responded: "OH, AGENT ORANGE, THAT EXPLAINS IT!" I was so overwhelmed that he recognized the damage that toxin had caused me that I burst into tears after he left the room.

As I have written in Chapter One, I was raised in a good Christian home. I never had any awful personal experiences. I did not have a stressful childhood history. That background made me more likely to develop PTSD since I had no life-altering experiences as a child or teen. This placed me between a rock and a hard place regarding escaping PTSD.

When a person has PTSD, they can become easily angered without warning and any apparent cause. I have that issue. One side effect of it is a super active response to unexpected sounds. A sudden loud or soft noise causes me to jump out of my skin. I know other Vietnam vets who have the same problem.

A significant problem with PTSD is how long it can last. One can deal with it to minimize the effects, but it lingers on and on. A level of recovery requires constant, demanding, and long-lasting work on the victim's part. "Talk therapy" was the primary way to learn to deal with my family and me during my therapy. For the first time in 40 years, I talked about the war and heart disease in a way never before during my first session. It was beneficial. It might be thought that reliving those horrible days would be counterintuitive, but it was a tremendous help.

Initially, upon returning home, I did not want to talk to anyone about my experiences. As the years passed, I became more open to addressing the matter. Unfortunately, very few people were interested in hearing my story. Often, when the subject came up, the listener would seek to change the subject. That was the exact opposite of what I needed to begin the arduous effort of climbing Out of the Night.

I have found talking to fellow Vietnam vets to be incredibly helpful. Talking about it in sessions with Elaine has been very helpful. She listens carefully and is fully engaged in the discussion. Recovery from trauma is not the same as recovering from an operation where the body completely heals.

Getting over traumatic events is not the likely outcome. People have said that they wish I could "get over it." That is not going to happen. What can and has happened is that I have learned to deal with what has happened to me. I have proceeded to have a productive and useful life.

Purchase additional copies of

Casualties of War
An Infantry Lieutenant in Vietnam

At these locations

www.lulu.com/spotlight/dshollar
www.amazon.com

Wherever books are sold

Contact the author at
ReadMyBooks2050@gmail.com

About the Author

David Hollar has spent most of his life in the Washington, DC metropolitan area, first in northern Virginia and then southern Maryland since 1973. He earned a B.S. degree from Bob Jones University in 1967 with a major in accounting. He married his wife, Sylvia, in July of the same year.

David served three years in the U.S. Army and reached the rank of First Lieutenant. His service included a year as an infantry platoon leader in Vietnam. He worked for a year as an auditor for Arthur Andersen & Co., and in 1971, he accepted a position as an accountant with the federal government's General Services Administration (GSA). He earned his C.P.A. certificate in 1973. He remained at GSA as a supervisory accountant until his retirement in 2005.

David and Sylvia have one son, Mike, and four grandchildren, Ben, Reagan, Tommy, and Grace. They live in White Plains, Maryland, and are members of the LaPlata United Methodist Church in La Plata, Maryland